SHANNON
Through Her Literature

Clonard House, Mullingar, headquarters of the Midland Regional Tourism Organisation (Lakeland), through whose area over eighty miles of the Shannon's waters flow

SHANNON

Through Her Literature

Padraic O'Farrell

THE MERCIER PRESS
DUBLIN & CORK

The Mercier Press Limited
4 Bridge Street, Cork.
24 Lower Abbey Street, Dublin 1.

ISBN 0 85342 699 6

The Author and Publishers wish to acknowledge the assistance received from:

Midland Regional Development Organisation (Longford, Westmeath, Laois, Offaly, Roscommon)
Lakeland – Midland Regional Tourism Organisation Ltd.
Bank of Ireland
Mullingar Pewter
Prince of Wales Hotel, Athlone
Rustic Oil Products – Jet Distributors
Cavan County Council
Roscommon County Council
Tipperary (N.R.) County Council
Galway County Council

and the support of:

Athlone Cruisers Ltd.
Longford-Westmeath County Library
Offaly County Library
Donegal-Leitrim-Sligo Regional Tourism Organisation
Shannonside Tourism
Shannon Development
Bórd Fáilte Éireann
Cork/Kerry Tourism
Kerry County Library
Leitrim County Library
Leabharlann Contae Cabhán
Holsten – Pils.
Bórd Iascaígh Mhara

Acknowledgements

I wish to record my sincere appreciation to the firms and institutions who assisted this publication (listed opposite), together with their staffs, for exemplary courtesy and consideration.

Generous encouragement and co-operation were always forthcoming from the National Library, Trinity College Library, Oliver Snoddy of the National Museum, Longford-Westmeath Library, Dick Roche *(Irish Independent)*, Fergus Linehan *(Irish Times)*, Jimmy Spollen *(Westmeath-Offaly Independent)*, Michael Killeen, Longford County Manager; Very Rev. F. R. Bourke, Dean of Killaloe; Frankie O'Gorman, John Conway, Harry Lynch, Simon Tormey, Matt Talbot, Hilary Hough, Col J. P. Kane, Shane O'Connor, Anne Coughlan, Seán Ó Súilleabháin, Matt Nolan, Seán Ó Rioghbhardáin, Seamus Hunt, Gerry Barry, David Errity, Michael Keegan, Paddy Collins, Billy Gilligan, Clive Brooks, Comdt Paddy Walsh and Eileen Clancy, as well as from the many lock-keepers, rivermen and country people who responded to questioning from a stranger in their midst.

I thank my wife, to whom I dedicated this book, and my family who were patient and understanding; Niamh typed the manuscript and must, therefore, get special mention.

The author and publishers wish to thank the following for use of copyright text, drawings and photographs:
Bórd Fáilte Éireann – The Irish Tourist Board, Midland Regional Tourism Organisation, the National Gallery of Ireland, Longford-Westmeath Library, Commissioners of Public Works, Ireland, Shannon Development, Shannonside Tourism, Electricity Supply Board, *Irish Times,* Joan Yourell, Gerard Kiely and John Conway.

FOR MAUREEN

Contents

Setting Out

PICTURE IRELAND as a craft at sea on a south-bound course. Mizen Head is leading and guiding, its modulating accents comparable to the rise and fall of the prow. The port side is the east coast, closest to the bright lights and pleasures. The west coast lies to starboard, far from the same attractions — often depressed, deprived and neglected, yet with access to the rarest vistas. North is the stern, a turbulent, throbbing engine-room below — explosive if not tended with care.

This leaves the midlands amidship. The solid, steady part of the deck was once regarded by mariners as sacred, and coursing through the midlands is a numen breathtaking in its beauty and grandeur: the magnificent River Shannon.

Here is a physical feature which vindicates grammarians who bestowed upon rivers the feminine pronoun. Whether flowing quietly, angrily, or with a sparkling wink, this *speirbhean* charms and edifies her most casual acquaintance. A prolonged glance can bring on an affection as durable as the hills and valleys, woodland and plains over which the great lady presides.

The Shannon was once a symbol of oppression. Oliver Cromwell was here from August 1649 to May 1650, during which time he broke the back of an Irish resistance that had been active since 1641. 'The Curse of Cromwell', 'To Hell or to Connaught' — the era of the slogan had arrived long before the introduction of hardboard placards and aerosols.

Again, in 1791, the Belfast Society of the United Irishmen demanded separation from England. Protestant Peep-o'-Day Boys began to victimise and harass Roman Catholics who formed a movement known as the Defenders to carry out counter-terrorist activities. Yet again notices warned Catholics to move across the Shannon. Le Chevalier de la Tocnaye, a French émigre, noted in 1796: 'I often met some of those wandering families on the way, the father and mother were carrying their movables, and such children as could not walk on their backs, followed by the other children who were also loaded with furniture, accompanied by the faithful pig and even by some poultry.'

'To Hell or to Connaught' was once more the warning, the Shannon again the great silver selvedge.

Present-day folk, happily, regard the Shannon as a haven for carefree pleasure craft. Its towns and villages are vibrant ports of call for happy holidaymakers renewing contact with creature comforts as well as old friends,

9

singing songs with strangers, swapping stories with *seanchaí* for, far from being extinct, the Irish storyteller is still a reality. He may now sit astride a high stool at a chromium gilded counter rather than squat on a creepy-stool by the hob. He may clasp a glass of vodka instead of a mug of buttermilk and poitín. He may even have his hand on a jeaned limb, God help us, rather than on a bog-oak rosary partnering a nugget of plug in a homespun pocket. But his craft remains the same, and he loves it as did his forefathers. It matters little to him if his audience is one or a dozen. While there is a listener he will perform. The verb is carefully chosen, for the Irish storyteller is as skilled an exponent of his own art as were F. J. McCormack, the Fay Brothers or Arthur Shields of theirs. If there is no new story to tell, there is a verse to recite or a passage from a great writer to quote, even a lie to tell.

The lordly Shannon has provided inspiration to many such *scéalí*, poems and books. Some authors came from far distant places to pay homage in the written word to the wonderous watercourse. Others lived close to her banks and wrote about other subjects when they tired of eulogising their goddess. All shared the soothing experience of dwelling for a moment or a year in the solitude that slumbers in her rushy callows or of admiring the splendour of her vegetal surrounds. This is the state in which creativity stirs.

The Source

Like all great and sacred Irish institutions, the Shannon is born in controversy. As if in doubt, the ordnance survey map spreads the legendary 'Source of the Shannon' across an area equivalent to a good Irish mile (a considerable, if ill-defined, measure!) of the Cuilcagh mountains in Cavan. About six miles above Lough Allen lies a deep, dark pool called Lug na Sionna or the Shannon Pot, which is usually considered to be the source. Geological experts say that a number of streams filter through the limestone surrounding the Pot and potholers claim to have found a definite source three miles from the Pot in County Fermanagh.

A County Leitrim lake once laid claim to being the Shannon's source. Loudly did Leitrim inhabitants sing their derisive song:

> So lordly, so solemn, so wondrous and grand,
> As she winds her sweet way through the length of the land;
> Lough Avanny's her source – doubts I pray have you not;
> Could such splendour emerge from old Cuilcagh's black Pot?

Seanchaí are, however, far more romantic. They say that a disciple of Manannán Mac Lir, god of Irish waters, had a daughter named Sionnan who

The Pot

craved a mortal education. She sought the Salmon of Knowledge. A strange and unapproved notion this, for women of the time were supposed to possess virtue, not wisdom.

Sionnan approached the Well of Connla wherein lay the intellectual fish. She attempted to catch it by the poacher's belly-tickling method, a downright insult to an esteemed salmonidae. With fin and tail it splashed water from the well and such was its power that great streams were formed. Nine of them flowed beside Nine Sacred Hazels, racing in pursuit of the fleeing Sionnan. They overtook her, drowned her and cast her body into the Land of Mortals through a large hole in the earth which is still said to have no bottom – Lug na Sionna.

Disputed sources in County Cavan are not confined to great rivers. The roots of Breifne's great men also arouse argument. One such man is Philip Henry Sheridan, hero of the American Civil War, described in a *London Daily News* obituary of August 1888 so: '[He was] not only the greatest cavalry officer of the Civil War, but he was also both a tactician and a strategist, capable of the most extensive combinations, and able to carry out far-reaching plans, and he had the nerve, resource and decision for emergencies that were wanting to some of the greatest strategists. . . He was one of the most soldierly soldiers of his time. He united brilliant courage, which he owed to his Irish origin, to the perfect steadiness and presence of mind in

11

Setting out from the Pot

emergencies.' It was men like Sheridan who acquired for our people the tag – then a proud one – of *The Fighting Irish*.

Somerset, Ohio and Albany, New York all lay claim to General Sheridan. Birth documents are missing, but all this matters little to the proud people of Killinkere where his father owned the first spoke-wheeled cart in the district. They insisted that he was born in their village. Having studied 'Fighting Phil's' equestrian statue in Washington, Padraic Colum eulogised the warrior in a ballad.

Spailpíní

Arthur Loftus Tottenham built houses at Glenfarne for the Sligo-Leitrim and Northern Counties Railway of which he was first chairman. The houses were collectively known as 'Slated Row'. The line, now extinct, was used to transport the Aberdeen granite pillars to the site of St Clare's church.

Underpaid workers, *spailpíní*, travellers from another parish or county – these were used for this type of toil. They would get a sum of money and 'dietem', that is a day's 'diet' (food). Here is the story of one such *spailpín*, luckier than most:

> The Sligo-Leitrim's office stands in lovely Lurganboy,
> The line itself a good two miles away;
> So Michael got his ticket, seized his satchel and his loy,
> And hoped he would be back another day.
>
> Belcoo, Glenfarne and Manor – he could try them all or no,
> The *spailpín* with a turf-bank in his eye;
> The lads from Slated Row would advise him where to go
> Once he promised them a *cliabh* when it was dry.
>
> Or perhaps he'd take ten shillings and dietem for a week,
> To haul Saint Clare's new pillars up the hill;
> But the Scottish granite's hard and he's carryin' too much lard,
> And what's more, no builder gives a man his fill.
>
> The evening down is rumbling into lovely Dromahair,
> A cottier spies the turf-man looking sad –
> 'Jump off here and come with me, and we'll share a pot of tea.
> Stay here the night, my hearty *spailpín* lad.'

13

So he stretched the night and more, on a pallet on the floor,
Cut turf by day then ate and slept till dawn;
And it also came to pass that the cottier's comely lass
Had Michael ogling like a love-sick fawn.

Then soon the pair were wed and of them it can be said
None ever were so happy or so fine;
And Michael he blessed the day he left Lurganboy to stray,
The day he rode the Sligo-Leitrim line.

The village of Dowra in County Leitrim stands vigilant above Lough Allen. The wording is carefully chosen for it was from here to the tip of the lake that the ancient frontier of Ulster ran. Legend told that the Black Pig's Race was formed by a porcine monster snorting and ploughing its way through the earth. A contemporary rhymer longs for the pig's return:

From Dowra to Kilgarriff in the happy days of yore,
The Black Pig's Race or Worm's Ditch stood seventeen-feet-four.
A stout fortification, big hog's horns upon its dome –
Let's build it up again and keep the Orangemen at home.

Ballinaglera, Co. Leitrim

14

Lough Allen

Our mountains gave birth to the Shannon
Which down through its valleys does plough
It spreads out white waves on Lough Allen
And washes old 'glera's fair brow

MYLES McTIGUE – LEITRIM POET

Like a pair of hands clasping a bright crystal pendant, two parishes girdle most of Lough Allen's shores. North and north-west is Inishmagrath, curving around to the Shannon a mile from where it enters the lake. Across the river is a neck of Ballinaglera parish which spreads to caress the upper eastern shore. So the Shannon and its extension into Lough Allen is the boundary line between the parishes.

Inch Island, called Inishmagrath on the ordnance survey map, paradoxically lies in Ballinaglera parish. In 1856 its landlords were the Lord Bishop of Elphin, Kilmore and Ardagh, and Sam McGee – not the cremated one made famous by Robert Service, but a clergyman. The island's rateable value then was £2.10s.

Inishmagrath and Ballinaglera people often went by boat to Drumshanbo market. On Good Friday in 1831, as a heavily-laden craft was returning under the direction of Johnnie McFadden, a storm broke, the boat sank and fourteen lives were lost. The funeral of the victims to Kilbride was a grief-stricken event and is commemorated by these lines, composed at the time:

The wild fowl of the water, no more they'll come to shore;
The blackbirds and the thrushes will all quit Mount Allen's grove.
The tree, in June, no more will bloom but wither and decline
Since Johnnie and his comrades took their lodging in Kilbride.

Of the many customs associated with holy wells, that of St Brigid's at Greaghnafarna is most unusual. To obtain favours a pilgrim was obliged to avoid shaving or polishing his shoes on a Sunday. Hardly fitting for a county said to have the highest percentage of its population in the priesthood and religious orders. Such is Leitrim's claim, and Ballinaglera means the town of the clergy.

There are many tales told of its holy men. 'Racey' Reynolds was a cleric renowned for his sprinting. Father Charles, to give him his proper title, once hid from his English pursuers in a deep dark chasm. Local historians are not sure of the century but they are certain of the priest surviving huge rocks and stones cast down into the darkness to annihilate him. Satisfied that they had wiped out their victim, the soldiers departed, remarking that even a cat would not survive their lapidary bombardment. The place has been called Poll a' Chait ever since. Prior to that, the fleet-footed-father was said to have been chased seven miles by his pursuers before leaping the Shannon itself. He shrugged off the amazement expressed at this magnificent feat with the remark, 'Ah but sure I had a good run at it — seven miles or so!'

Theophilus O'Flynn was a *seanchaí* and poet-blacksmith from near Drumkeeran. Born in 1770, he emigrated to the United States having spent some time as a wandering bard. Some of his songs are preserved in the Royal Irish Academy, many with notes attached. One of these notes, written by Hardiman, reads: 'Twenty-nine songs, good, bad and indifferent as they are from the dictation of that eccentric old Scealaidhe, Theophilus O'Flynn. Some of them are excellent, ten of Carolan's.' It must be assumed that Hardiman was not casting aspersions on Carolan's music!

An inlet of Lough Allen known as Tommy Simpson's Lake had a smelting furnace in which ore from Sliabh an Iarainn (Anierin) was man-handled by barefooted labourers. Pikes for the 1798 rebellion were fashioned there. The manager of the furnace, anticipating the arrival of the Yeoman who raided it, fled his premises loaded not with pikeheads but with the takings in gold accrued over a long period. He threw a sack of the precious metal into Tommy Simpson's Lake.

Arigna coal fuelled the smelter then. Its valleys still supply power generated from an Allenside station to a land where a pike has disappeared but the reason for its use remains.

Drumshanbo to Carrick-on-Shannon

Moonshine, dear moonshine, oh how I love thee,
You killed my poor father but I dare you try me;
Oh bless all moonshiners, and bless all moonshine,
Sure its breath smells as sweet as the dew on the vine.

TRADITIONAL CHORUS

A visitor to Drumshanbo in 1825 had this to say: '. . . I was informed that the people were in a state of despondency and dismay, at the interruption of their trade in illicit spirits, by the vigilance of the new police; for it had been not unusual, some time before, to see several hundred kegs of smuggled whiskey brought into the town for sale in open day, at the markets. Illicit distillation was not over at this period, however; and the frequency of the practice may be judged of, when I add, that in one morning's excursion over the mountains, I saw no less than five stills, all busily at work in different places. I doubt that I should have observed them, so obscure and so well concealed were the spots which had been chosen for the operation, had it not been for the guide who accompanied me, and who, of his own accord, invited me to turn my spy-glass in the right direction. Fire, pans, tubs, still were all in an instant distinctly under my eye. On asking the guide how he could have ventured to point out these doings to me, a stranger, who might give information, he replied with a roguish archness, "Oh! Sir, good care was taken to find out what was bringing you to the mountains, or may be you would not have been allowed to pass so peaceably over them."

'In fact all the people were in league...

'A few minutes afterwards we descried from the heights a party of police spreading over the bogs below, as if in pursuit of game. "They are all wrong, they are all wrong," cried the fellow joyfully; and they did in fact make a totally false cast. . .'

Few Irish poets have had the courage to condemn drink. On the contrary, poetic excitation — Shannon's excepted! — is regarded as being less than potent if it is not born of an alcoholic amnion.

The Irishman who commits a slight sexual indiscretion is a downright sinner, for the pillars of his society have deemed the land's seven deadliest sins to be – in descending order of gravity: Adultery, Fornication, Flirtation,

Gardaí destroying a still

Mixed Bathing, Kissing, Walking Out and Holding Hands.

But the drunkard — now that's a different thing entirely! — at worst he is classed as 'a holy-terror'. A Leitrim poet, John Keaveney, passed sentence on the drinking habit in a self-criticism entitled:

THE LAST AND BITTER GLASS

Weak and helpless now I stand at old and hardened age.
I've travelled o'er life's woeful ways and stopped at every stage.
The songs of sots and revelry oh yet I think I hear,
Which hurries down my furrowed cheek and a salt and scalding tear.

At twenty years I entered into manhood's coarse career,
I followed fickle fancy, which cost me twice too dear,
In every vice indulging and virtue did not know,
Which daily draws me deeper in the graceless ponds of woe.
. . .

At thirty years a wooing went, to change a dreary life,
I took then into partnership a kind and gentle wife,
Resolutions they were made, of course were made in vain,
The temple showed some sweetness where but bitterness remained.
...

At forty years a failure and daily growing worse,
I can't extract a copper from a gold forgotten purse,
Dissension is the dagger by which I alleviate,
The hardships of a family without a bite to eat,
The cries of little children around my aching head,
A brutal blow is my response, take that instead of bread,
I hasten from their presence as senseless as an ass,
To beg or borrow openly, the Last and Bitter Glass.

John Keaveney was born in Brackery about 1844, one of the famine years. A hedge school-master named 'Mickey the Master' taught him, and some say he succeeded his mentor, setting up school in his own home. Poor eyesight, they claim, prevented his being incorporated into the National School system.

He gave his full support to the Sinn Féin movement. A young man, Charley Dolan, was a prominent local leader within that organisation. His older poetic colleague, wrote like a true champion of liberty in praise of Dolan and his cause:

CHARLEY ÓG SINN FÉIN

Today our hopes are higher than they have been in the past,
The sun of Independence beams down on us at last,
No more the land of bondage, of trial and of tears,
The brutal hand of tyranny forever disappears.

Abroad there is a lady fair; Miss Freedom is her name,
The Harbinger of Liberty, the Faculty of Fame,
Monarchs all admire her, she dwells in France and Spain,
The foster sister of a youth called Charley Óg Sinn Féin.

19

Bartley Harrington with posthorn and bag

20

She left this land of ours some centuries ago,
Her noble soul unfit to bear with Sarsfield's overthrow,
She brushed her golden hair aside, she turned and beheld,
The savage herd of horse and foot by which she was expelled.

Grattan sought and found her out and brought her back again,
To make the land more happy and to help her to remain,
But villians sold her to the foe for titles and champagne,
Which leaves the true heart bleeding of Charley Óg Sinn Féin.

But her ladyship is coming for she is too long away,
Sycophants and critics are the cause of her delay,
But when she comes with fifes and drums, we'll tell the world plain,
That we wish success to her sweet self and Charley Óg Sinn Féin.

Bartley Harrington was a postman around the middle of the nineteenth century. Every day of the week except Sunday, he walked from Leitrim village to Ballyfarnan and back with his posthorn, mailbag and umbrella. An anonymous balladeer wrote of him:

M 50,020/914/17

> Bartley Harrington came on with his sack on,
> Through stones and stiles and wintry miles.
> The people of Leitrim came out to meet him,
> Saying, 'Tarry, dear Bartley, with your letters a while.'

From 1793 to 1797 one Myles Gerald Keon recruited throughout north Connaught for the United Irishmen whenever he was free from his pleasant duties as patron of the County Leitrim Harpers whom he accompanied to musical festivals throughout the land. Harpers were always respected by the gentry for lampoonery was greatly feared by them. As a titled gentleman, Keon may not have been fully trusted or approved by his Leitrim kinsmen, yet Wolfe Tone said of him and of his zeal on behalf of Catholic Emancipation: 'It is to the sagacity of Myles Keon of Keonbrooke, County Leitrim that his country is indebted for the system on which the General Committee was to be framed anew, in a manner that should render it impossible to bring it again in doubt. . .'

Myles' grandson, bearing the same name, was born into the Carrick-on-Shannon home in 1821 but was orphaned at the age of six. His grandmother cared for him until her death and then his uncle Count Magawley, sometime

Susan Langstaff Mitchell from a portrait by John B. Yeats.

Premier of Maria Louise in the Duchies of Parma, Gaustalla and Placentia, continued the task. Myles received a Jesuit education at Stoneyhurst, spent a period in France and in her army before returning to England to study law and literature. Perhaps it was his army service that evoked his tribute to soldiers contained in his classic novel *Dion and the Sibyls,* published in 1866. His remuneration for the two volume work retailing at one guinea apiece was £20.

The Geographical Distribution of Irish Ability contained an unfortunate allegation attributed to one D. J. O'Donoghue who died in 1917. It went: 'It is difficult to say why Leitrim should be the lowest of all counties in intellectual achievement but such it is.' Strange, for more than a century earlier Wakefield's *An Account of Ireland, Statistical and Political* had commended the people for their attitude to their children's education: 'In every direction cultivation was creeping upwards. I saw women employed in milking cows until noon, and it gave me no small satisfaction to find that the children, instead of being left to saunter about in idle groups, were universally sent to school.'

Carrick-on-Shannon poet Susan Langstaff Mitchell, who did most of her writing about the turn of the century, certainly belies Mr O'Donoghue's accusation. She left the Leitrim town when her father, a bank manager, died. A friend and journalistic colleague of George Russell (AE), her artistic leanings were towards poetry of which she had three volumes published. Some of her verse was of a religious nature:

> Age cannot reach me where the veils of God
> Have shut me in
> For me the myriad births of stars and suns
> Do begin
> And here how fragrantly there blows to me
> The holy breath,
> Sweet from the flowers and stars and hearts of men,
> From life and death.
> We are told, O heart, we are not old,
> The breath that blows
> The soul aflame is still a wandering wind
> That comes and goes;
> And the stirred heart with sudden raptured life
> A moment glows...

Of her home town she wrote:

> I will not walk these roads of pain.
> I will turn back to youth again.
> 'Tis full sunlight though past the moon
> The night will not come very soon
> And if you haste we may lie down
> Before sunset, in Carrick town.

After her own sunset in 1926 at the age of sixty, AE wrote of her in the *Irish Statesman* — of which she had become sub-editor in the year of her death — that she was 'one of the best Irishwomen of her time, capable of following the profoundest thinking and of illuminating it by some flash of her own intuition. . .'

> We're safe before the sun goes down
> And sleep is sweet in Carrick town. . .

Freemasons of Carrick-on-Shannon

Concord Lodge 834 of the Freemasons of Carrick was originally an Itinerant Lodge, the chest with the paraphernalia of the brethren being brought from one venue to the next. Abraham O'Connor, Past Provincial and Senior Grand Warden of north Connaught, who was Secretary of Concord Lodge, reported that in 1802, 'the Warrant comes to Carrick for a thirteen months' stay, and the Lodge was held in Mr O'Beirne's. . .'

The building of proper and permanent premises was long deferred. Because of famine and disease, as O'Connor's report later states, to comfort the dying, '. . . rescue the perishing and feed the hungry are duties of far greater importance than building of halls; and I am proud of the Brethern of 834 for their noble efforts to relieve the sufferings of their fellow-beings at this period. . .'

He was reporting on the year 1864, when famine times were ending.

Carrick-on-Shannon from the air

Boyle and the Boyle Waters

BEFORE any sailor, traveller or wayfarer passes further downstream from Carrick-on-Shannon he must recognise the fact that the Boyle Waters, extending north-west from the town, are considered by most men of the river to be as much a part of her as is the bard, Carolan of her history.

Few dispute any decision to probe the diversion, for Lough Key's beauty is famed, her surrounds renowned for historical and legendary heritage. Since most of this small county has already been traversed by a trip on the Sligo-Leitrim line it would be parsimonious to neglect the area of which it is said that flora akin to that discovered in the Himalayas is found.

A Statistical Survey of the County of Roscommon by Isaac Weld, published by the Royal Dublin Society in 1832, lauds certain sociological aspects of Boyle town. A comprehensive report includes the following passages: 'From one extremity of the island to the other, possibly, no establishment exists in a town of the same size, provided with so great a variety of articles, or in so extended a scale as the shop and warehouse of Mr Mulhall. . .

25

'Really it is refreshing in this land of murmuring and repining, to see what may be effected, when industry and prudence, judgement and enterprise, go hand in hand. Yet. . . in by far the greater number of shops I entered in Boyle, complaints were common of the stagnation of commerce and decrease of the country trade. It was an unvarying tale, that the peasantry who frequented the town were poorer than formerly; at least, that they did not spend money as they heretofore used to do. . .

'One, and only one shop, appeared exclusively for millinery and haberdashery near the bridge, as usual a lounge for the younger branches of the military in garrison, where the whiff of the cigar was seemingly not prohibited of a summer's evening at the open doors. I merely noted this because it has appeared to me from long observation both at home and abroad, that a milliner's shop is a sort of test of the gaiety of the place. Wherever these magazines of female fashions abound, and are well provided with novelties, a sure inference may be drawn that gay ladies exist in the place, and pleasure is afloat. . .

'I saw but one watchmaker's window in Boyle, and that on a very humble scale, merely as an appendage to other business. This seems to speak poverty;

Boyle town

26

but the Irish are early risers and count time by habit, with tolerable exactness. Yet the great value of time is, in general, to be learned in Ireland. . .'

Begging was a problem too: 'As the carriages drove off, a cry or shout was commonly raised by the throng; of gladness from those who had received, of bitterness and reproach from those who had not. I recollect one morning early, a fine carriage, with four beautiful bays, handsomely appointed, driving up to the door, from which three young men alighted to breakfast. A gilded mitre shone on the panels. Rapidly did the intelligence spread, and an immense crowd of beggars gathered to share the expected bounty. . .

'I was assured, that certain persons high in rank and station, were actually deterred from entering into the town of Boyle, excepting upon urgent occasions, by the crowds of beggars, and the gross language with which those were frequently assailed who did not respond, by the amount of their alms, to the expectations which had been formed. . .'

St Attracta and the Celtic Cross

The Abbess Attracta was a contemporary of St Patrick from whom she received the motto 'Hospitality and Charity Towards All'. Boyle, being then a place where seven roads met on the highway, was selected by her manservant, Mochain, as an ideal location on which to build a hospice for travellers, thus gaining for the town the distinction of having the first commercial hotel in the

Begging peasants, 1847

Boyle Abbey

land. Its grade is not known but its tariff was remarkable. Everything was free! And to those who will argue that it was not, therefore, a commercial hotel, supporters of the theory retort by saying her recompense was the currency that all Ireland could understand: goodwill.

The internationally recognised Celtic Cross originated during a visit to the hospice by St Patrick. According to *The Book of Armagh:*

'It is related that when St Patrick came to Boyle to ordain priests and consecrate bishops for various missions he paid a visit to the new building of St Attracta. The good woman was pleased to have this opportunity of having the place blessed by the apostle himself. . .

'When everything was in readiness it was discovered that the paten for the celebration of Mass was not at hand. St Patrick was about to defer the ceremony when Attracta interposed, telling the saint that God would provide the missing paten. He did so.

'The preparation for the Sacred Mysteries had hardly commenced when a golden disc appeared above the head of St Attracta and gently rested on her shoulders as she bent in silent prayer. Taking the mysterious gift she reverently ascended the steps and placed it on the altar. The paten was found

28

to be incised with a Cross, wrought within a circle. St Patrick, it is told, taking it is his hands, said: "It is clear that the Lord God has listened to thy prayers, and it is evident that the image which this paten bears must be preserved, because it is given thee from on high. This holy cross shall receive its name from thee, and the Irish shall hold it in veneration, as thou has surpassed so many others in sancity. . ."'

Turlough Carolan

The barony of Boyle saw the greatest concourse of harpers ever assembled in Ireland when they gathered for the four-day wake and funeral of the harper and composer Turlough Carolan in 1738.

Born in Nobber, County Meath in 1670, he moved at an early age with his family to Ballyfarnon. The MacDermott Roes befriended them and Carolan was educated with their children until he became blind, at which time Mrs MacDermott Roe had him taught to play the harp. She provided him with a horse, a servant and money when he was twenty-one, and he set out on his career as a wandering harper.

Isaac Weld assembled information received from Daniel Eardley, an acquaintance of the bard, from near Arigna: 'Carolin [sic] had a literary education, and had pursued his studies with diligence up to his eighteenth year; he then had the misfortune to catch the small-pox, and to lose his eyes *[Most commentators say Carolan was blind at fourteen years of age]*. Previous to this calamitous event music had not engaged his attention; he turned to it as a solace in his misfortune, and he began with learning the harp. The want of early practice, however, to supple the fingers, marred his progress on that instrument, so that he was never able to acquire rapidity of execution. What he attempted to play in public, nevertheless, was always performed with correctness and neatness.

'At twenty-one he began to compose; and his first essays gave such promise of success, that his masters recommended him to direct his whole powers to composition, rather than to vain endeavours to attain excellence on his instrument.

'His first poem, a mock-heroic one, was entitled "Shee-more and Shee-beg", occasioned by a quarrel between two gentlemen of the country, in which there had been *cannonading* amongst the factions on either side. It was set to music, and the reputation which it immediately acquired for Carolin, encouraged him to undertake compositions of a similar nature. He was caressed by the gentry and at each house wrote verses and composed music in praise of those whose bounty he partook. Living thus in the midst of plenty and good cheer, Carolin got gradually addicted to strong liquors, and at last became a confirmed drunkard. A day seldom passed over without intoxication. He drank spirits habitually without any admixture of water. . .

'His name is still fresh in the memory of the people of the surrounding country, and the spot is pointed out with confidence by the villagers, in which his bones had been deposited, although they have long since been jostled out of the place originally assigned as their last home, in the contentions for similar accommodations for other claimants. Still some respect had been shown to his remains; they were not absolutely scattered to the winds; and a skull, supposed to have been the identical one that had been the seat of music

Carolan

and of verse, was placed in a niche within the walls of the old church, where, decorated as a mark of distinction with a black riband, it received, in grim and ghastly state, for many years, the adoration of the gaping crowds at the annual *patterns*.

'But oh! most foul of deeds; the skull was snatched away at last by the daring hand of a monger of curiosities. This was before the time of phrenology, so that the theft had not even the pretence of scientific research to palliate it. Whether, however, the cranium had ever actually stood on the shoulders of Carolin, seems altogether problematical; though it is said the officiating grave-digger swore to its identity, of his own special knowledge. . '

30

While going to Mass one Sunday Carolan is said to have met a cetain Miss Fetherston, possibly a daughter of Thomas Fetherston of Ardagh whose country home is featured in Oliver Goldsmith's play *She Stoops to Conquer*. (The bard was often entertained by the gentry and he wandered over a sizeable area.) The chance meeting perhaps inspired his lines:

> On a fair Sunday morning devoted to be
> Attentive to a sermon that was ordered for me,
> I met a fresh rose on the road by decree,
> And the Mass was my action, my devotion was she.
> 'Welcome bright angel of noble degree,
> I wish you would love and that I were with thee,
> So pray do not frown at me with mouth or with eye' –
> So I told the fair maiden with heart full of glee
> Though the Mass was my motion, my devotion was she.

Such unashamed admission of lukewarm enthusiasm for the Sacrifice was rare at the time. Not so was the composer's inclination for honouring women with his lyrics. It was for Mary MacDermott, daughter of the Princess of Coolavin, the MacDermott's Princess Royal, that he wrote *The Princess Royal*. But he also wrote for great men: *Donnchadh Mac Cathal Óg*, for example, lauded Denis O'Connor who always extended great hospitality to the itinerant bard.

Turlough Carolan, composer of the air used for *The Star Spangled Banner* and a number of planxties adopted by Thomas Moore, died on 25 March 1738. He is commemorated by a festival in Kilkeeran and by an inscription over the entrance to Kilronan cemetery which reads: 'Within this churchyard lie the remains of Carolan, the last of the Irish bards who departed this life 25 March 1738 RIP.' (Nowadays the bard's grave is clearly marked and an 'O' bestowed upon his surname.)

Lough Key

> When Carolan plucked his old high G,
> All the lads in Gorteen they did flee;
> For he played off Lough Arrow,
> Off lovely Lough Gara,
> But he never played it off Key.

Lough Key

Around Lough Key in the late seventeenth century, lived 'the three most hated men in Ireland': William Sidney Clements, Earl of Leitrim and the colonel of the Leitrim Regiment of militia; Lord Kingston of Kilronan, reputedly one of the most cruel landlords in Ireland; and Colonel King-Harman of Rockingham House near Boyle.

Now in ruins, Rockingham House was described enthusiastically in the early nineteenth century by Isaac Weld: 'One of the most striking features of the house consists of its perfectly insulated position, no office of any description being visible; but the whole being surrounded by smooth shorn grass, interspersed with beds of flowers and ornamented walks. This arrangement has been affected by having most of the offices of the basement storey covered over, and subterranean passages carried from underneath the eminence on which the house stands, towards the lake in one direction; and in another towards the stables, which stand at a considerable distance screened out by trees; the covered passage, however, does not reach the whole way to the latter, but merely far enough to prevent the appearance of movement near the mansion. . .'

32

How the servants felt about their underground existence is unrecorded. They were at least better off than tenants on the Rockingham estate. Forced to carry manure from the stables to the fields in basketwork creels strapped to their backs, they would work all day soaked to the skin with the rancid contents.

The shores of Lough Key were the scene of an early ecumenical meeting. As is common in many parishes, there were Protestant and Catholic 'plots' side by side in a small cemetery near Ardcarne. An intolerable occurrence came about when the foot and ankle of a long buried Colonel Kirkwood released itself from its interred state and protruded into the grass on the Catholic side. A meeting was called, eventually, between the parson, the priest and a local farmer credited with great wisdom. He had the sagacity to arm himself with a bottle of whiskey for attending the discussion.

The three sat upon a fallen yew and surveyed the trespassing limb. They passed the bottle around and the solutions were tendered after each swig. The parson and priest soon forgot their ecclesiastical problem and began discussing the price of 'motoring cars' while the wise farmer continued staring at the foot with a cogitative countenance. Noticing how the clergymen were ignoring the problem, he stood and before leaving the cemetery was heard to remark, 'Well, if that's the way they look after their business, old Kirkwood has as good a chance with one as with the other'.

Percy French

Before leaving the vicinity of Boyle, there is a man of the next barony who must be accorded a welcome in any book on the writers of the Shannon.

William Percy French, that lovable, laughable rascal of Irish entertainment, might well have received his bubbling, effervescent wit from the Shannon's eddies as she took an occasional diversion to encircle a ruined castle or an historic mound, the more to enhance her charm.

The man who was 'born a boy' in Cloonyquin, County Roscommon and 'remained one' until his death at Formby in Lancashire is most famous for his songs 'Phil the Fluther's Ball' and 'Are ye Right There, Michael?' – a satire on the West Clare Railway. As a young engineer, however, he joined the Board of Works in 1881 and became Surveyor of Drains in County Cavan:

Percy French

34

Let others betake them to Western Plains
And ease the redman of his ill-gotten gains;
No tomahawk ever shall injure the brains
Of William, the Local Inspector of Drains.

He mounts his tall trap, gives his charger the reins,
And gallops away through the green country lanes,
The Board pays the posting – the balance remains –
With William, the Local Inspector of Drains.

He finds out the holding and what it contains,
Then maps out his system in furlongs and chains,
And points out positions for 'miners' and 'mains' —
Such wisdom has William, Inspector of Drains.

He plunges through marshes long haunted by cranes,
Unmindful of how the dark bog-water stains;
Traducers assert that this ardour he feigns,
They little know William, Inspector of Drains.

He stays in his quarters, of course if it rains,
And wakes the piano's voluptuous strains,
And if of delay the bold tenant complains,
He's sat on by William, Inspector of Drains.

The fair maids of Cavan (this William maintains),
Tho' I think one should take it with salt, a few grains,
Have left in a body their woe-begone swains
For William, the Local Inspector of Drains!

'Tis an onerous post – but the writer refrains
From dwelling at length on its pleasures and pains,
It may not last long, but as yet he remains
                    Yours faithfully,
                        William
                 Inspector of Drains.

   Percy French's songs and parodies won him world acclaim, but he was also a prolific writer of short plays, sketches and dialogues.

East Roscommon

From Jamestown to Lanesborough, the Shannon forms one boundary of an east Roscommon area once known as Trí Tuachas or Three Districts. Tir Briuin na Sionna, Cinel Dobhtha and Corca Eachlinn met at Grange bridge and each had a distinguished history. The last of the Firbolgs, that small doughty, bandy brigade, dwelt here in the Sliabh Baghna hills. Here also Bald Michael, a direct descendant of Muircearthacht Mór Mac Earca, high king of Ireland, received his name with his monkship and was a celebrated professor of divinity from the North Swampy Plain around Clooncullen.

In this area, as in Leitrim, the tradition of the Cake Dance survived longest. Various interpretations of this intricate piece of Celtic choreography were performed, some indoors, many outdoors – all associated with prandial prancings of one kind or another. Reverend James Hall, in his *Tour Through Ireland,* published in 1813, wrote: '[I]t is no uncommon thing to see groups dancing on the roads and by-corners, on Sundays and holidays, after prayers; no house being able to contain the numbers which, in fine weather, generally meet on these occasions.

'It often happens that some innkeeper. . . sends a loaf, of less or more value, not exceeding five shillings, to be given as a premium to the best dancer; in other words, to the person who spends most money at the inn. Many times the young men spend more than they can spare, to have the pleasure, and, as they esteem it, honour of dividing the loaf among the dancers. . .'

Most descriptions of the event, however, include the loaf impaled on a staff stuck in the earth amid garlands and ribbons and danced around with great gaiety by abandoned youth, kept merry by a nearby ale-wife.

Some say the term 'He takes the biscuit', describing someone outstanding, originated at the Roscommon Cake Dance.

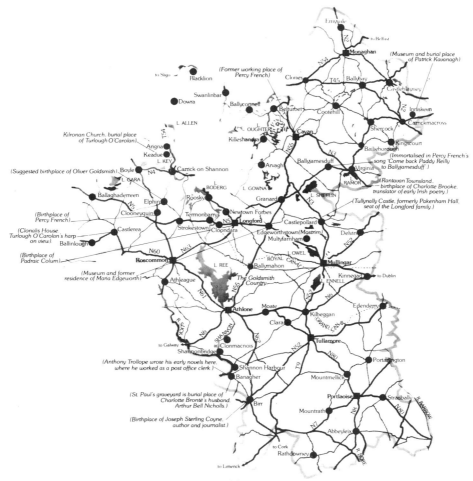

A Literary Map of the Upper Shannon

Into Longford

A NOTICEABLE lack of trees, a marshy plain, little of interest — that's how Shannon's Longford shores are usually dismissed by the noteworthy writers. If they are proceeding down river they are promised too many attractions below Athlone. If pursuing an upriver course, they hurry on to where the Drumsna Dún causes the Shannon to flow north at Jamestown (for the only time in its course).

However, the Shannon is the heart of the midlands and Longford is a typical midland county. It is only fair to wander inland to Edgeworthstown

The only place the Shannon flows north

and the home of two writers, Richard Lovell Edgeworth and his daughter Maria.

Richard Lovell Edgeworth is better known for his inventive genius and for being the father of Maria than for his writings. He is said to have installed an early hot-air heating system in Pakenham Hall, the first such innovation in a country house in Ireland. He spearheaded bog drainage and reclamation near the Shannon and invented a semaphore system. Politically, he was an advocate of Catholic emancipation and a Volunteer supporter. A father of twenty-two children (three dying in infancy) and a man of rare honesty, he maintained: 'I am not a man of prejudices. I have had four wives. The second and third were sisters and I was in love with the second in the lifetime of the first.'

Richard Lovell Edgeworth was born at Bath in 1744 and educated at Oxford. Maria, his second child, was born at Black Bourton, Oxfordshire in 1767 and she too was educated in England. When she was fifteen years of age the family moved to Edgeworthstown where she assisted her father in his scientific pursuits and the management of the estate, as well as taking a hand at educating the rest of the children.

Mr Edgeworth had many ideas which were in advance of his time. In 1798, when some would expect him to have been otherwise engaged, he was co-author with his daughter of *Practical Education*. *Professional Education*, which he wrote in 1809, outlined a form of training similar to the present-day vocational system. Other fruits of their collaboration, often with the purpose of explaining the Irish and Hiberno-English language to English readers, were more lighthearted. For example, in 1807 they published an *Essay on Irish Bulls*. '*A laughable confusion of ideas* creates a bull,' they wrote, and went on to relate a tale of 'Paddy Blake's Bull':

'When Paddy heard an English gentleman speaking of the fine echo at the lake of Killarney, which repeats the sound forty times, he very promptly observed – "A Faith that's nothing at all to the echo in my father's garden, in the county of Galway; if you say to it – "How do you do, Paddy Blake?" it will answer, "Pretty well, I thank you, sir."'

Maria Edgeworth

They also offer some still-good counsel pertinent to Shannon's foreign visitors: 'We must not from false delicacy to our countrymen, here omit a piece of advice to English retailers or inventors of Irish blunders. Let them beware of such prefactory exclamations as – "By my shoul and St Patrick! By Jasus! Arrah Honey! My dear Joy! etc." because all such phrases, besides being absolutely out of date and fashion in Ireland, raise too high an expectation in the minds of a British audience, operating as much to the disadvantage of the storyteller as the dangerous exordium of – "I'll tell you an excellent story;" an exordium to be avoided by all prudent wits.'

Anthony Butler, author and journalist, asserts that Sir Boyle Roche (1743-1807) was the father of the Irish bull, but concedes that he was born long after the birth of his child. Roche is famous for a prime beef bull which the Edgeworths quote without garnish (or credit): 'What has posterity done for me that I should do so much for posterity?' Possibly the Edgeworths had him in mind when they wrote: 'There is one distinguishing peculiarity of the Irish bull – its horns *are tipped with brass*. It is generally supposed that persons who have been dipped in the Shannon are ever afterwards endued with a supernatural portion of what is called by enemies impudence or assurance, by friends self-possession or *civil courage*.'

Although it must be admitted that the distinguished duo are guilty of retailing what must be one of the earliest Irish jokes – about 'the Irishman, who begged a friend to look over his library, to find for him the history of the world before the creation. . .' – their attitude was generally admiring. There is nothing like a bit of praise to hold the attention.

'The Irish nation from the highest to the lowest in daily conversation about the ordinary affairs of life, employ a superfluidity of wit and metaphor which would be unintelligible to a majority of the respectable body of English yeomen. Even the cutters of turf and drawers of whiskey, are orators; even the *cottiers* and *gassoons* speak in trope and figure. Ask an Irish *gassoon* to go early in the morning on an errand, and he answers, "I'll be off at the flight of the night".'

Of course, the Edgeworth name is most famous for Miss Edgeworth's novels, the first and best known of which, *Castle Rackrent,* was published in 1800. Maria Edgeworth pioneered nineteenth century Anglo-Irish fiction and was greatly admired by Sir Walter Scott, who wrote: 'I felt that something might be attempted for my own country of the same kind as that which Miss Edgeworth so fortunately achieved for Ireland.'

A product of the Anglo-Irish ascendancy, she chronicled their foibles, failings and foolishness. In doing so she provided a faithful and lasting memorial to these people and their ways – a testimonial to a class now virtually extinct. Miss Edgeworth was also, of course, extremely well acquainted with and knowledgeable about the other strata of society in the Longford Shannonside area. Some of her footnotes to *Castle Rackrent* are entertaining and illuminating:

'*Middlemen*. — There was a class of men, termed middlemen, in Ireland, who took large farms on long leases from gentlemen of landed property, and let the land again in small portions to the poor, as under-tenants, at exorbitant rents. The *head-landlord*, as he was called, seldom saw his *under-tenants;* but if he could not get the *middleman* to pay him his rent punctually, he *went to his land, and drove the land for his rent;* that is to say, he sent his steward, or bailiff, or driver, to the land to seize the cattle, hay, corn, flax, oats, or potatoes, belonging to the under-tenants, and proceeded to sell these for his rents. It sometimes happened that these unfortunate tenants paid their rents twice over, once to the *middleman,* and once to the *head-landlord.*

'The characteristics of the middleman were servility to his superiors and tyranny towards his inferiors: the poor detested this race of beings. In speaking of them, however, they always used the most abject language, and the most humble tone and posture – *"Please your honour, and please your honour's honour"*, they knew must be repeated as a charm at the beginning and end of every equivocating, exculpatory, or supplicatory sentence; and they were much more alert in doffing their caps to those new men than to those of what they call *good old families.* A witty carpenter once termed these middlemen *journeying gentlemen.*

'*Vows* – It has been maliciously and unjustly hinted that the lower classes of people in Ireland pay but little regard to oaths; yet it is certain that some oaths or vows have great power over their minds. Sometimes they swear they will be revenged on some of their neighbours; this is an oath that they are never known to break. But, what is infinitely more extraordinary and unaccountable, they sometimes make and keep a vow against whiskey; these vows are usually limited to a short time.

'*English tenants.* – An English tenant does not mean a tenant who is an Englishman, but a tenant who pays his rent the day that it is due. It is a common prejudice in Ireland, amongst the poorer classes of people, to believe that all tenants in England pay their rents on the very day when they become due.

'*Weed-ashes.* – By ancient usage in Ireland, all the weeds on a farm belonged to the farmer's wife or to the wife of the squire who holds the ground in his own hands. The great demand for alkaline salts in bleaching rendered these ashes no inconsiderable perquisite.

'*A raking pot of tea.* – We should observe, this custom has long since been banished from the higher orders of Irish gentry. The mysteries of a raking pot of tea, like those of the Bona Dea, are supposed to be sacred to females; but now and then it has happened that some of the male species, who are either more audacious, or more highly favoured than the rest of their sex, have been admitted by stealth to these orgies. The time when the festive ceremony begins varies according to the circumstances, but it is never earlier than twelve o'clock at night; the joys of a raking pot of tea depending on its being made in secret, and at an unseasonable hour. After a ball, when the more discreet part of the company has departed to rest, a few chosen female spirits, who have footed it till they can foot it no longer, and till the sleepy notes expire under the slurring hand of the musician, retire to a bedchamber, call the favourite maid, who alone is admitted, bid her *put down the kettle,* lock the door, and amidst as much giggling and scrambling as possible, they get round a tea-table, on which all manner of things are huddled together. Then begin mutual railleries and mutual confidences amongst the young ladies, and the faint scream and the loud laugh is heard, and the romping for letters and pocket-books begins, and gentlemen are called by their surnames, or by the general name of fellows! pleasant fellows! charming fellows! odious fellows! abominable fellows! and then all prudish decorums are forgotten, and then we might be convinced how much the satirical poet was mistaken when he said – There is no woman where there's no reserve.

'The merit of the original idea of a raking pot of tea evidently belongs to the washerwoman and the laundry-maid. But why should not we have *Low life above stairs* as well as *High life below stairs?*'

The Absentee was first written as a play about landlords and tenants. Maria's father attempted to have it staged in London but the Lord Chamberlain would not license it, deeming it an imprudent theme to offer at the time. Producers, furthermore, felt they would experience some difficulty finding actors for so many Irish characters.

For any that fish the waters of the Shannon there is advice in *The Absentee* from Count O'Halloran: 'The count, to reconcile matters, produced from an Indian cabinet, which he had opened for the lady's inspection, a little basket containing a variety of artificial flies of curious construction, which, as he spread them on the table, made Williamson and Benson's eyes almost sparkle with delight. There was the dun-fly, for the month of March; and the stone fly, much in vogue for April; and the ruddy fly, of red wool, black silk, and red capon's feathers.

'Lord Colambre, whose head was in the burial-place of the Nugents, wished them all at the bottom of the sea.

'"And the green-fly, and the moorish-fly!" cried Benson, snatching them up with transport, "and, chief, the sad-yellow-fly, in which the fish delight in June; the sad-yellow-fly, made with the buzzard's wings, bound with black braked hemp, and the shell-fly, for the middle of July, made of greenish wool, wrapped about with the herle of a peacock's tail, famous for creating excellent sport." All these and more were spread upon the table before the sportmen's wondering eyes.'

In spite of her somewhat quaint interpretations of Irish folk custom and the

The Rectory, Edgeworthstown

behaviour of her own class, however, Maria Edgeworth did point out the tyranny and hardships to which tenants were subjected by malevolent landlords. She also attempted to defend the badly vilified Irish character. Richard Lovell patronised eight schools in Edgeworthstown and the village had a remarkably high standard of education. The family home is still serving the Irish nation as Our Lady's Private Nursing Home.

Before departing Longford, another Edgeworth must be mentioned, Richard's cousin Henry Essex was born at Edgeworthstown in 1745, the son of a Protestant rector who later converted to Roman Catholicism. Henry was ordained a priest in a French order and, because the French found Edgeworth too formidable for pronunciation, he became known as the Abbé de Firmont. (Firmount lies north of Edgeworthstown.) He heard the last confession of Louis XVI and attended him at the guillotine before his execution in January 1793. After his escape to England, he refused appointments as bishop to several Irish dioceses and the presidency of Maynooth. The Abbé de Firmont died of fever contracted from French prisoners of war in Mittau in 1807.

Lough Ree

I'm sad and I am lonely now in this far off west,
The happy scenes of bygone days at night disturb my rest;
For in this faithful heart of mine forgotton ne'er can be,
The days I spent with Molly Bawn, a-boating on Lough Ree.

She was young and tender, far prettier than the fawn;
Her eyes they shone like diamonds bright or the stars of early morn.
A smile she had for everyone but her kisses all for me
Entranced I gazed on Molly Bawn, a-boating on Lough Ree.

She pledged herself to be my bride, how happy then was I;
How dulcet were the joys of love, how quickly they flew by,
But heaven's light shone in her eyes, she was too good for me,
An angel marked her for his own, and took her from Lough Ree.

I've crossed thro' many a thorny path, my hair's a silvery hue;
Yet her thrilling voice speaks in my heart, in tones I can't subdue.
Her comely form still haunts my mind, her pleasing face I see –
The blushing face of Molly Bawn, a-boating on Lough Ree.

44

'Leo' Casey

The song about Molly Bawn, sometimes Mary Bawn, was learned by children of the midlands long before it was assumed to be a sample of the writings of John Keegan Casey. Known as 'Leo' this poet, who made his name with the fiery ballad *The Rising of the Moon,* was born at Castletown-geoghegan, County Westmeath. As a youth in Gurteen, County Longford, he assisted his father at teaching and he continued that occupation for a decade before he started writing poetry. As James P. Farrell wrote in his *Historical Notes of County Longford* in 1886: 'There was at this time in Ballymahon a real true-hearted *Soggart aroon,* named Father Lee. To him Casey applied for permission to start a Purgatorian Society in the parish. Father Lee knew Casey well – knew him from his boyhood – and readily gave his consent to the formation of a society for so charitable an object. The society was easily formed – everyone knew and everyone loved "Leo" – and ere long he had all the young men, and some of the staid men too, in his Purgatorian Society. But after each night's meeting, the scholars used to wonder how it was that the seats would be piled up in a corner, and the floor cleared. They thought that if the *Dies Irae* was being chanted, the society should be seated, or if the Rosary were being recited they should kneel – for neither of which positions would it be comfortable to have the seats piled in a corner; and so gradually it came to be tacitly understood that whilst "Leo" and his brother-members were doing good for the souls of the dead, they were also thinking of doing good for those who were living – in other words, "Leo" was a Fenian organiser; and what safer way could he take to make converts?'

'Leo' and the 'Bard of Thomond' (Michael Hogan) engaged in many verbal jousts through the correspondence columns of *The Nation*. In quoting both Casey and Hogan this work may bring the peace of Shannon upon their souls!

The Lake and its Islands

Lough Ree is not the most suitable place for invoking peace for that lake can be choppy and squally and it can resound to rifle-fire from the army ranges at Carnagh. Yet the lake drew superlatives from many writers, among them one R. Harvey who, in 1896 expressed himself thus in *The River Shannon and Its Lakes:* '. . . Some of the islands also bear fine trees. The best wooded one is Hare Island, near the Westmeath shore, at the southern end of the lake, the property of Viscount Castlemaine, who has converted it into pleasure-grounds, and constructed a fanciful cottage residence, embowered within the old trees. There are some ruins of religious houses here, founded by the family of Dillon, some of whose descendants still live in the neighbourhood. The remains of antiquity both military and ecclesiastical, along the shores of Lough Ree, are peculiar sources of interest, standing as monuments of the predilection which the ancient inhabitants of the country entertained for the confines of this beautiful sheet of water, whether in reference to the strength of certain places as military positions, or to the calmness and retirement which others afforded for the purpose of religion and devotion.'

Hodson Bay, St John's Bay, Inchmore, Inchturk, Nun's Island – Mr Harvey praises them all before he concedes: 'But the gem of all these islands is Inishclauraun, or, as the old poet says:

> Seven and twenty beauteous islands,
> Which I shall name in proper order
> According to their size and dignity.
> And first of all, I would like to mention those famous islands
> On which I find, as authors mention,
> That holy men placed dwellings
> Therein to worship the King of Glory.
> I shall visit Inis Cloethrinn,
> Which exceeds all the others for beauty
> It was on this isle of grass and beauty
> That Maeve of Croghan, Queen of Connaught,
> Fell by the son of the King of Madh
> On the time of war and of bloody murder!

But because a Quaker named Mr Fairbrother built a summer house on the island, it became known as Quaker Island and Clothran, the sister of Queen

46

Church ruins and early Christian grave slab on Inchcleraun

47

Maeve, was forgotten.

If contemporary writers and many from the near past avoid elaboration on Ree's tempestuous nature, not so *The Four Masters* who noted, concerning the shipwreck 'of Dealbhna Nuadhat on Loch Ribh, with their Lord Duimasach. . .: Thrice nine vessels and three of the gamhawraighe of Loch Ribh, there escaped of them from life, except alone the crew of one vessel.'

The Four Masters also tell of the wreck of O'Conor and Sil-Murray in 1190.

R. Harvey does mention Lough Ree's habit of becoming turbulent without warning, in a pleasant piece of folklore: 'Some years ago a young gentleman from County Roscommon spent a day on Inis Cleraun; and, towards evening, put out in his boat, with a companion, for the mainland. One of the sudden squalls, so frequent in the Lough, came on; the men lost control of their boat, which was overturned; and, though one of its occupants managed to reach the land, the younger sank and was drowned. For days the lake was dragged for the body, but no sign of it could be found.

'About ten days after the sad ocurrence Mrs Farrell was in the field beside the Clogas Church, busy milking her cows, when, amongst the trees shading the ditch she suddenly heard what she describes as 'the sough' (a sobbing, mournful sigh) of a voice, which seemed to move, wailing as it went, all along by the ditch from Grianan Maeve down to the very water's edge; here, at the beautiful little bank, the voice rested – as if the owner were standing still – bewailing.

'The listener was terribly frightened; and, hurrying home, told what she had heard. Her husband and another man crossed to the place where she declared the voice she had heard had paused; and at that very spot they found the body of the unfortunate youth who had been drowned. It had just been carried ashore.

'It is certain that it was under these circumstances the body was discovered, and no one who lives upon Inis Cleraun has ever doubted that it was the Banshee whose wail was heard as she issued from the old home of Queen Maeve, and treaded her way along the stones from the Grianan down to the lake, where sometimes, even in the broad noon, a figure, believed by some to be Saint Dermot, is seen to walk over the waters, as if on dry land. . .'

Diarmaid was St Ciaran's teacher. He founded a monastery on the island in the sixth century. Giolla na Naomh O'Farrell, King of Annally, was buried there in the twelfth century. It was the aforementioned Ciaran who sailed down the Shannon to found Clonmacnoise.

A celebrated Ballymore correspondent to the *Westmeath Examiner* called James Woods wrote a work beloved of all who ever 'saw the sights from

Uisneach'. He included a substantial history of the Westmeath shore of Lough Ree. Excerpts from his narrative read as follows:

OLD LOUGH REE

'With its numerous islands, rich in historic association and full of glorious traditions of the past, stretches for miles from Athlone to Lanesboro', and is a favourite haunt for the angler and antiquarian. Innisboffin, Inchmore, Hare Island and Saint's Island, what memories do they not recall — saints and sages, poets and bards, warriors and scholars, who frequented its shores and enjoyed the hospitality of the pious recluse who far from vanities of life, practised austerities, and kept the faith alive, despite tyrannic statutes, the bribe and the halter.

KILKENNY WEST

'A monastery was erected here about the middle of the sixth century by St Canice, which was called after him, Cill-Channaigh, and from which the parish and barony derive its names. . .

'The debris of ruined castles and monastic edifices are profusely scattered about this neighbourhood. There is a holy well in the locality dedicated to St Canice. In old times the festival was celebrated on the 11th October.

'Hare Island, anciently called Inis-Aingin, is situated in Lough Ree, near the Shannon. A monastery was founded here about the year 542 by St Kieran, who, to distinguish himself from the other saints of his name, is usually called the Son of the Artificer, patron of Clonmacnoise. This great saint was born in the ancient Kingdom of Meath, received his early education under St Justin, one of St Patrick's disciples, and then entered the celebrated school of Clonard, where he graduated for some years under the learned founder, St Finian. From Clonard he went to the monastery of St Nonnidius, in Lough Erne, and subsequently we find him in the great monatery of St Enda, in the isle of Aran, Galway Bay, whither he went to improve himself in the knowledge and practice of monastic discipline. At the expiration of seven years he entered St Senan's Abbey of Inisheathy, whence he removed to Hare Island where he erected a monastery, which was soon filled with holy monks. He governed Inis-Aingin for six years, and then he founded the celebrated monastery of Clonmacnoise, which in after years became one of the most famous of our Irish religious foundations.

LOUGH REE AND ITS ISLES

'Old Lough Ree, what glorious traditions and associations surround thee! The murmuring of thy gentle waves, like the voices of the past, telling, as it

49

were, secrets of the great deeds of the historic dead. The surface of the lake in the summer presents to the eye of the tourist a long series of glittering waves, rising and falling in sluggish undulations, and rolling in languid procession towards the shore. . .

'The banks of Lough Ree witnessed many a hard fought battle between the Danes and native Irish and not infrequently rival chieftains and their respective followers; and its tranquil shores were often crimsoned with the blood of the virtuous and true, shed by the sacrilegious despoilers and desecrators. . .

INISBOFFIN

'This is an island in Lough Ree, and the name signifies the "island of the white cow". An abbey was founded here about the end of the sixth century, by St Rioch, bishop and abbot. The *Four Masters* have the following notices of this place:– 750 – Fiangalach, Abbott of Innis-bo-finne, in Lough Ribe, died 809 – Blathman, Abbott of Innis-bo-finne, died 916 – Feardhach, Abbott, died 1089 – Munstermen plundered the churches of Lough Ree, including Innisboffin.'

In coursing southward through centuries the Shannon encountered more benign Munstermen than those early eleventh century aggressors, for her route passed by monasteries, churches, chancels and other places of great sanctity. But for connotations of reverence few places can compare with a sheltered spot three miles above Athlone on the lakeshore. Once the site of the first Poor Clare nunnery in Ireland, the hallowed haven bears the name Bethlehem.

Castle and harbour, Athlone circa 1910

50

Athlone

ATHLONE, at the southern end of Lough Ree, has through the centuries been an important military site on the Shannon. The Uí Maine kings had their site there as far back as the tenth century. In 1129 Turlough Mór O'Conor, High King of Ireland and King of Connaught, built a large fort for the protection of the bridge he had erected there. The Anglo-Normans built the motte-castle on the Connaught side to secure the river crossing after they seized it in 1199.

Even in times of relative peace, as towards the end of the reign of Edward I, the gorget that is the Shannon at Athlone was a turbulent strait indeed. A state roll of 1301 observed: 'Because the Irish. . . on each side of the water of the Schyen, make from day to day a great multitude of boats with which they take divers preys on the King's land in the parts of Randon and elsewhere upon the King's faithful men being at peace, and it is feared that worse may happen by such malefactors who continually remain in the parts of Athlone where the entrance is very narrow into the King's land of Connaught: It is agreed. . . that a galley be made of at least 32 oars which shall constantly remain at Randon, for the defence of the castles of Athlone and Randon if it shall be necessary.'

Later, Elizabeth I found it necessary to detach herself from attempting to negotiate a marriage between herself and the brother of the King of France in order to issue *Fiat Ire, No. 1666* (15 January 1571): 'Appointment of Christopher Davers of Killenaghe, gent., to be chief sergeant and water bailiff on the river Shenan, and the loughs Rye and Halye from their heads as far as they be portable to the rock of Astenan near Limerick. Recites that the great number of boats and cots on the river facilitated robberies from the banks. . . The bailiff has authority to destroy upon the finding of 12 honest men, all unnecessary boats, none to be allowed on the river without his brand, and is to have two galleys to scour the river, one above and one below Athlone.'

Warfare on the Shannon

As 1690 came to a close a fleet was proposed for Williamite forces on the Shannon. According to a document entitled *A true and impartial history of the most material occurrences in the kingdom of Ireland* published three years later. . . the lord justices 'ordered four longboats, like men-of-war's pinnaces, to be fitted up with patteros and little small guns, the sides to be fortified with boards and other materials, and those to be fitted with a hundred choice men, commanded by Captain Hoord, who had been provost marshal, but turned out for some irregular things, and was resolved to do some desperate service to be re-admitted. These boats were to be drawn upon carriages to the Shannon, and there put in; the design was very plausible, and might have done service if pursued; for there are several islands in the Shannon, wherein the Irish have very considerable riches; and besides, Hoord and his men designed to make incursions into the enemies' country, and to burn and destroy all before them; if a small party appeared, then they would fight them, but if a great body, then they could retreat to their fleet, and go away to another place. And further, one design of those boats was to carry over a part of our army (at least their necessaries) that shortly designed on expedition beyond the Shannon; but the boats were stopped beyond Mullingar, and ordered to go no further.'

The Shannon's most celebrated action was undoubtedly the second siege of Athlone when Sergeant Custume called for ten men to die with him for Ireland and got a hundred volunteers. With crowbars, mallets and pick-axes, the party threw themselves upon the beam of the bridge to break it down but went under to a fusillade of gunfire and grapeshot before their work was complete. Another party took their place and completed the work, again sustaining a number of casualties, many of them fatal.

Almost every Irish schoolchild learned Sir Aubrey de Vere's stirring poem about that action which took place in 1691:

> Does any man dream that a Gael can fear? –
>   Of a thousand deeds let him learn but one!
> The Shannon swept onward broad and clear,
>   Between the 'leagures and broad Athlone.
>
> They wrenche'd at the planks 'mid a hail of fire:
>   They fell in death, their work half done:
> The bridge stood fast; and nigh and nigher
>   The foe swarmed darkly, densely on.
>
> 'O, who for Erin will strike a stroke?
>   Who hurl yon planks where the waters roar?'
> Six warriors forth from their comrades broke,
>   And flung them upon that bridge once more.
>
> Again at the rocking planks they dashed;
>   And four dropped dead; and two remained:
> The huge beams groaned, and the arch down-crashed –
>   Two stalwarth swimmers the margin gained.

St Ruth in his stirrups stood up and cried,
    'I have seen no deed like that in France!'
With a toss of his head, Sarsfield replied,
    'They had luck, the dogs! 'Twas a merry chance!'

O many a year upon Shannon's side
    They sang upon moor and they sang upon heath
Of the twain that breasted that raging tide,
    And the ten that shook bloody hands with death!

To this day Sergeant Custume is remembered in Athlone, and its army barracks, the headquarters of the Western Command, is called after the gallant soldier. The name was bestowed by Commandant General Seán Mac Eoin in an effort to avert near-mutiny among his men after they had taken over the establishment from the departing British in 1922. When anti-Treaty elements were proving troublesome, Mac Eoin appealed for a symbolic re-enactment of Custume's deed in saving Athlone, and named the barracks after him.

British troops vacating Athlone Barracks in 1922

In Weld's 1832 survey of the County Roscommon there is a description of the military barracks which leads into a few lines about its hospital: 'Dr Strean remarks, that the medical staff had found, heretofore, that the troops, on arriving at the barracks were very commonly affected with diarrhoea; but, since this was not a disease which prevailed as an epidemic in Athlone, its occurrence was attributed to the situation of the general hospital, which heretofore was placed so close to the river, that in winter, the walls were washed by the current, and, in summer, exposed to the effluvia arising from putrid animalculae, and aquatic vegetables, when the waters receded. The most peculiar disease, latterly prevalent amongst the troops quartered here, consisted, as I was informed, of ophthalmia, arising, as it was believed, in great measure, from the glare of light reflected from the gravel and walls, without any relief.'

Sir William Wilde, who in 1851 published a book on the *Epidemics of Ireland,* visited Athlone barracks to investigate this recurring phenomenon. Commenting on Athlone's general climate, he said it was the dampest he had ever experienced except during the rainy season in India.

Weld was more concerned with the town's deplorable bridge, the worst on the whole river almost: 'It is not merely a discredit to the town alone, but a positive stigma upon the nation. The breadth of the road does not exceed twelve feet, whilst the length of the bridge amounts to one hundred yards; consequently, carriages cannot pass each other without great difficulty, and when once fairly entered upon the bridge there is no retreating. . . [O]n market days, and when there are fairs in the vicinity, more particularly during the great cattle fair of Ballinasloe, human beings, cattle, cars, carriages, are so closely wedged, that the passage becomes an affair of absolute danger as well as inconvenience. What might not be the peril to a military division, if ever there happened to be an occasion for a retreat across it?'

In 1838, too, the town and the bridge got unfavourable mention, this time from Leitch Ritchie, Esq.: 'You cannot walk in the streets of Athlone: you must wade. So inconceivably dirty a place does not exist in Europe, and the broad streets are as filthy as the narrow ones. On my return from the bridge, I walked up the main street, through which the country carts were crowding, four abreast, two on the causeway, and one in each troittoir; and it may be imagined that, even by tacking from side to side, and creeping under the horses' necks, I made but slow progress. I understand that the actual governor of the town is very generously, though by no means *justly* rewarded for his negligence or incapacity.

'A new bridge has been talked of for some years; but I fear there is no chance of the plan being carried into execution. The commerce of the river seemed to me to be nearly confined to turf; but I heard that considerable quantities of corn were exported. . .'

The author went on the describe 'one of the most beautiful little fortresses I ever saw at home or abroad. . .', while alluding to an affray between the towns people and the military. He endured a nineteenth century 'mugging' too: 'I was knocked down by some of the inhabitants, who came behind, and struck me so earnest a blow on the back of the head with a bludgeon, that my hat was cut through, as if with a knife. This compliment, which was followed by several others when I was down, I have reason to believe, was intended for one of the officers of the garrison, and I hope the gentleman will excuse me for intercepting it. . .'

North of Athlone is Goldsmith country. Controversy ever surrounds the poet and playwright and arguments about his place of birth are seldom settled satisfactorily. Roscommon folk claim Smith Hill House, Elphin, home of Oliver's maternal grandfather, while Longfordians adhere to the more widely accepted belief that he was born in Pallas.

The man's 'Irishness' is questioned too. Some regard him as English merely because his father was a parson! They say that, far from being around Auburn or Lissoy, County Westmeath, the 'loveliest village of the plain' stood in Wiltshire, England.

> Sweet Auburn! loveliest village of the plain;
> Where health and plenty cheered the labouring swain,
> Where smiling spring its earliest visit paid,
> And parting summer's lingering blooms delayed;
> Dear lovely bowers of innocence and ease,
> Seats of my youth, when every sport could please. . .

Now why should we try to will such poetry across the sea? Let us make up, drop into the nearby tavern and forget our differences:

> Then come, put the jorum about;
> And let us be merry and clever;
> Our hearts and our liquors are stout,
> Here's the Three Jolly Pigeons forever.

The 'Pigeons' is in Lissoy where a family relative, Elizabeth Delop, privately taught the boy whose father was rector at nearby Kilkenny West. Oliver went to the local village school when he was seven and there the budding genius of

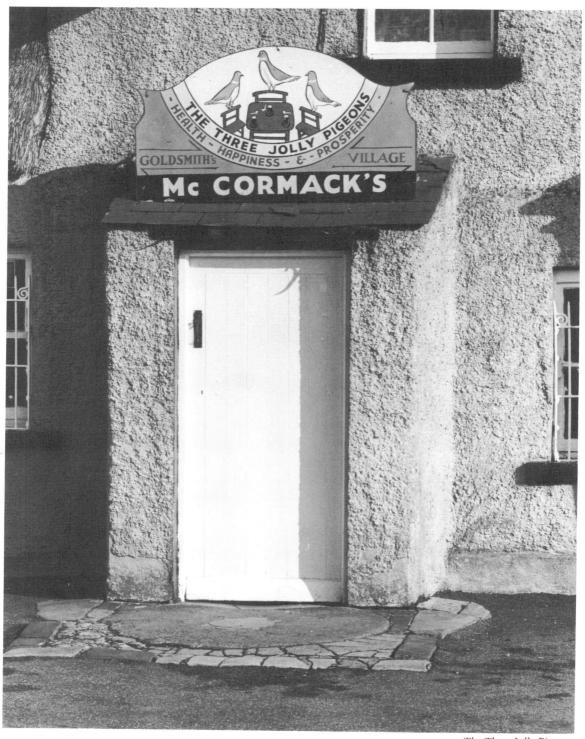

The Three Jolly Pigeons

Oliver Goldsmith

letters was instructed by a retired regimental quartermaster – still on half pay from the armed forces. Despite his service with the British army, this schoolmaster regaled the boy with stories about Galloping Hogan and Baldearg O'Donnell as well as tales of 'banshees' and other spirits of the Irish countryside.

Oliver, apparently, asked for more and he became very fond of traditional Irish music. He is said to have listened, at ten years of age, to the last notes played on the harp by the great Turlough Carolan, before the bard died.

In Goldsmith's play *She Stoops to Conquer,* the characters Marlow and Hastings are sent to Squire Fetherston's house by a practical joker who assures them that the 'old Buck's Head on the hill (is) one of the last Inns in the whole country'. This is based on an actual incident in the author's life.

While at school in Edgeworthstown (Mostrim) he hired a horse, borrowed a guinea and set out for Lissoy. At Ardagh, he acted the gentleman and inquired at a local inn as to where he might find a place where he could put up for the night. A local vagabond, Cornelius Kelly, directed him to the 'big house'. Eventually the laugh was on Kelly for Goldsmith made £500 during the first six week's run of the play based on the incident.

The Fetherston house in Ardagh became a College of Domestic Science under the care of the Sisters of Mercy. The village also boasts a tiny church in which is buried St Patrick's nephew, St Mel, (a revered saint of the diocese which derives its name from the village) who was made a bishop by Patrick. This beautiful spot, viewed from nearby Ardagh Hill, is seen to have a remarkable collection of churches in a tiny area.

Ruins of Lissoy Parsonage

Ardagh Hill was Bri Leith, one of the foremost fairy seats in the land and later an important Lughnasa Festival site. A giant was said to hunt there and stories of unexplained lights seen on the hill were as plentiful as stories of 'swallyholes' into which the giant could lure innocent children. Much of the legend surrounding the giant, Midir of the Sighe (or King Midas) and his wife Etain is concerned with Ardagh Hill. Etain was changed into an insect by a former wife of Midir. At an unhygienic royal table 1,000 years later the insect fell into a goblet of wine, was swallowed by a queen and was later born that queen's daughter. She eventually married Eochaid Airem, King of Tara and arrived back where she started when Midir won her off Eochaid in a chess game.

It was on such legends that Oliver Goldsmith was brought up.

In all my wanderings round this world of care,
In all my griefs – and God has given my share –
I still had hopes, my latest hours to crown,
Amid these humble bowers to lay me down. . .

. . . Down beneath the mythology and the serenity of a country-side worth rambling through, worth pausing within to reflect on life and its unfortunate new-found, almost unbearable pace, worth straying to – even from Shannon's majesty.

The Hill of Uisneach and the Birr Stone

On the Ballymore route from Athlone to Mullingar, there is little to indicate that a rise of ground on the left near Killare is one of the most historic spots in Ireland. It is difficult to believe that from the summit of this rise can be seen twenty counties – given a clear day – for the Hill of Uisneach is not imposing. It is merely an insignificant 602 foot slope in Westmeath's grasslands. Its richness in legends and tradition, however, is great and worthy of all the praise lavished upon it by historians, archaeologists and folklorists alike.

Lugh, divine father of Cuchullain, was said to have been slain there by three rival gods. A synod of bishops was held on its slopes in the twelfth century – some say it was one of our first cases of gerrymandering as they carved up the dioceses of the Kingdom of Meath. A century before, Brian Boru himself had downfaced Maelseaghlin the Second by encamping on the hill which was connected by carriageway to Maelseaghlin's own seat at Tara.

Uisneach had a very special Beal Festival, for the Rock of Divisions, Aill na Mireann, stood there. Now called the Catstone (because it looks like a cat's face from the road below) this great boulder got its Irish name because it was said to divide – or be the meeting point of – the ancient provinces of Ireland. Éire herself is said to be buried under it.

Back in the sixth century, during the reign of Diarmuid, son of Cearbhall, there was some discontentment among Ireland's noblemen because of the vastness of the royal domain. One chief, Fintan – '. . . set up. . . a pillarstone of five ridges on the summit of Uisneach and he assigned a ridge of it to every province of Ireland and he marked out the portion of each province. . .'

It takes but a simple effort to climb and examine more closely *Umbilicus Hiberniae,* as Geraldus Cambrensis called the rock. If we are to believe all we are told about Ireland's 'navels', however, we will have to accept that poor Cathleen Ní Houlihan is an absolute freak. The other chief contender for the claim is the 'Birr Stone' now standing in the town of that name and bearing the marks, we are told, of the very cock that crew when Peter denied Christ. It is

Aill na Mireann   *Bealin Cross*

not explained whether Birr cocks crow very loudly or Peter had keen hearing. Other tales say this was the stone of the Fianna and that the marks are those of Fionn Mac Cumhaill's fingers, made when he flung the rock after a thieving Scottish giant.

According to Thomas Dineley, who visited Ireland during the reign of Charles II, the stone was '. . . to be seen a quarter mile from Birr on. . . ye road to Dublin which seems to designate that part of the townland of Seffin where the G.S.W.R. railway now stands. [Furthermore] . . . Sergeant Isaac, an Innkeeper at ye White Hart conducts you to the sight of it.'

The Birr stone is five or six feet in diameter and has marks resembling the letter V, with crosses similar to those seen on pagan rocks at Clonfinlough, near Clonmacnoise on the Shannon. Dineley's journal continued: 'The stone itself was taken in December 1833, from its ancient site by the late Thomas Steele, Esq. (O'Connell's head Pacificator) on a truck drawn by eight horses, and was by him deposited at Cullawn, near Tulla, in the County of Clare.'

But the Claremen didn't reckon with the doughty midlanders and the stone, that had served as a Mass rock for a congregation which included Daniel O'Connell, was returned to Birr in 1955.

Ballymore

Heading back from our diversion we pass through Ballymore – the town with 'two inds and no middle', according to a west of Ireland traveller. The original

60

town was, we are told, submerged beneath Lough Sunderlin, later called Lough Seudy. James Woods carried an account of the incident in his *Annals of Westmeath:* 'In the good ould times, before the British connection or the steam engine was invented, or the telephone dreamt of, when every farmer and labourer ate his own pig, and before the praties got black, the town of Ballymore was situated a quarter of a mile north of its present position. The good citizens of the village had a never-failing supply of pure spring water from a well situated in the centre of the town. They were simple, unassuming people, and the idea of supplying themselves by artificial means, like their more polished descendants of the nineteenth century, was never entertained. In the middle of the well there was a large stone to stand on, which was very useful to fill pitchers and other utensils with the sparkling liquid. It happened at the time of the singular change, that there resided there a woman of the Paddy-go-easy type, one who was not very particular about her domestic affairs. One of her failings was that she had a weakness for washing the children's clothes and Paddy's shirt in the well, and pounding them on the stone with a wash-staff, to the great indignation of her neighbours, who had no redress save physical force, as there were no courts of law, or sanitary officer to admonish her; they were blessed luxuries unknown to our forefathers. Well, one morning, the legend says, she was at her job washing, when, on a sudden, to her horror, she saw water spring up about her in all

directions, and in a few minutes 80 acres of land was flooded, and ancient Ballymore disappeared forever.'

Early in the fifteenth century, the King's Lieutenant, John Stanley, assaulted Niall O'Higgins on Uisneach. Now Niall was the equivalent to an Irish Poet Laureate of the time. Despite the reputation of the hill for eliminating elegists, the aforegoing lines are offered in the hope that Uisneach will not erupt and cast St Patrick's Bed back across to Killare and into St Brigid's Well. But just in case — back to the Shannon, with perhaps a moment's delay at Twyford to inspect the interlacings, geometric patterns and deer-hunting scenes on the early ninth century Bealin cross.

Designs from Bealin Cross incorporated in pewterware handcrafted by Mullingar Pewter

61

Offaly's Shore

THE FAITHFUL County they call it. Often under-estimated, the staid, serene midland tract of bog and pasture sends forth few sons to sound trumpets. Clonmacnoise has such an effect on its visitors that they forget to ask what county claims it. Offaly people do not remind.

> Bellmount, Banagher, Ballycumber, Birr,
> The Offaly 'B's can create a stir;
> But the best for the cooking and the best for a man
> Is Hairy Maggy Mary from the town of sweet Ferbane.

Hairy Maggy Mary was only upholding the tradition which unequivocally states that Offaly women are the best in Ireland for attending to the needs of men. Limerick, they admit, has its share of beauties; Galway, they allow, has long-limbed dusky girls with a Spanish strain. But for gut satisfaction, nobody disputes the prowess of the Maids of Blackwater and Brosna. The Fianna, they say, had a rest-camp near Rahan. Where Jesuits now salve troubled souls, Offaly women once cared for weary warriors.

Offaly women are 'the souls of decency that would let you pick their pot till you could see the sun through it'. They have a tradition to uphold, of course, as we learn from L. M. McCraith of Loughloher, Cahir, in the delightful book *The Romance of Irish Heroines* published in 1913.

MARGARET O'CARROL – 'THE BOUNTIFUL'

'The mind loves to linger over the gracious picture of Margaret an Einigh – Margaret the Bountiful – which has been drawn for us by one who must have known her well. He was one of the long line of MacFirbis – the hereditary historians of Lecan – he was Margaret's contemporary, and, no doubt, one of her guests. Margaret O'Carroll was no cloistered votary like St Brigid, yet she was scarcely less pious. She was no queen like Gormflaith, no passionate princess like Dervorgilla, yet her influence upon the period in which she lived must have been as great, while it was infinitely more beneficent.

'*The Annals of the Four Masters* describe Margaret as "The best woman of her time in Ireland".

'Margaret's time was somewhat less disturbed than times which went

Margaret O'Carrol's Feast

before, and were to follow it. The Anglo-Normans had established themselves as conquerors, but in many cases had already become "More Irish than the Irish". The great Norman families, the Fitzgeralds, Butlers, Burkes, and the rest, had their feuds but these were not as prolonged as the Wars of the Roses, at this time occupying the English, and keeping them at home in England. In Ireland, this seems to have been a comparatively settled period, and one which saw a great revival of religion and letters.

'Early in the fifteenth century, Margaret O'Carrol, daughter of Tadhg, Lord of Ely, and of the O'Carrols, was married to Calvagh O'Connor, Lord of Offaly. We first hear of her as his wife, still under her maiden surname (as is even now the custom in parts of Ireland), mending highways, and making bridges, building churches, and providing Mass Books. It is written that she "made most, in her time, of all manner of things profitable to serve God, and her soul".

'Having regard to the travelling conditions of her day, perhaps the most remarkable event in Margaret's life — more noteworthy even than the Two Invitations of Margaret, which gave her the name of "the Bountiful" — was her famous pilgrimage to the Shrine of St James of Compostella in Spain, in the year 1445. The names of the principal pilgrims have been recorded, and chief among that "goodlie company of noble and ignoble" we find "the admirable Margaret O'Carrol".

'. . . Margaret O'Carrol was a women of culture and large mind, who loved and appreciated the society of the learned, and desired to do them honour. This is shown by the story of her "Two Invitations". The Mac Firbis historian who records it, or his father, or perhaps both of them, were among her guests.

'Mac Firbis writes: "It was she that twice in one year proclaimed to, and commonly invited. . . all persons, both Irish and Scottish, or rather Albains, to the general feasts of bestowing both meat and money, with all manner of gifts, whereunto gathered to receive these gifts and matter, two thousand and seven hundred persons (besides gamesters and poor men)."

'"These feasts were held on Lady Day, March 25th, and 'Lady Day in Harvest', August 15th, that is on the Feast of the Annunciation, and of the Assumption. They took place at the two ends of Offaly, at Killeigh, and at Rathangan, respectively. Margaret caused her husband's "chief judge", or brehon, to write out for her "a list of the learned Irish". These she invited and entertained, "clad in a gowne of cloth of gold, with her dearest friends about her, and her clergy, and her judges (brehons), too, Calvagh himself also, on horseback by the Church's outward side, to the end that all might be done orderly, and each one served successively. And first of all, Margaret gave two chalices of gold as offerings that day on the Altar of God Almighty. She also caused to nurse, or foster, two young orphans. We never heard neither the like of that day, nor comparable to it, in its glory, and solace. And the second day (at Rathangan) was nothing inferior to the first."

'Mac Firbis continues his quaint and eulogistic description until he comes to "Anno Domini, 1451, . . . an ungracious and inglorious year to all Learned in Ireland, both phylosophers, poets, guests, strangers, religious persons, soldiers, mendicants, and poor orders, and to all manner and sorts of poor in Ireland, because the general support of their maintenance's decease – to wit, Margaret, daughter of Thady O'Carrol, King of Ely, Connor Offaly Calvagh's wife, a woman that never refused any man in the world for anything that she might command, except only her own body. While the world lasts her many gifts to the Irish and Scottish nations cannot be numbered. God's blessing, and the blessing of all saints be on her going to Heaven, and blessed be he that will reade, and will heare this, for the blessing of Margaret's soul. Cursed be the sore in her breast that killed Margaret. . ."

'This glimpse, through the mists of more than five hundred years, is a very intimate one. We can visualise the bountiful lady in her golden gown. We can realise her as one full of practical usefulness and initiative, generous and appreciative, refined and virtuous.

'Thomas D'Arcy Magee has written some charming verses in praise of Margaret, and in description of her famous feast:

. . . Margaret, like our Lady's Self,
. . . unto the troubled land
Brings quiet in her holy smile, and healing in her hand.
It is not that her father is renowned through Innisfail;
It is not that her lord is hailed sentinel of the Gael;
It is not that her daughter is the wife of the O'Neil;
It is not that her first-born's name strikes terror thro' the vale;
It is not for all her riches, but her virtues that I praise.
She made the bardic spirit strong to face the evil days.
To the princes of a feudal age she taught the might of love,
And her name, though woman's, shall be scrolled their warrior names above.

Low lie the oaks of Offaly, Rath Imayn is a wreck,
Fallen are the chiefs of Offaly – death's yoke on every neck.
Da Sinchel's Feast no more is held for holy in the land.
No Queen, like Margaret, welcomes now the drooping bardic band,
No nights of minstrelsy are now like Irish nights of old,
No septs of singers such as then McEgan's book enrolled.

Shaft of North Cross with Teampull Finghin in the background

But the name of Margaret Carrol, who taught the might of love,
Shall shine in Ireland's annals even minstrel's names above.'

Yet it is not the name of Margaret O'Carrol nor any other of its women that makes Offaly a very special hinterland of Shannon. Rather it is a name that has graced the pages of the most respected volumes in the Christian world – Clonmacnoise – a placename that never fails to instil a sense of awe and reverence, however cynical or materialistic society has become.

The dawn chorus of songbirds has a peculiarly ethereal quality in Clonmacnoise. Here it is a *Gaudeamus* of avian freshmen praising the memory of a glorious scholastic past as grey stone slowly and sombrely comes frowning out of the night to front young day's arrival in pink and orange party ribbons.

The Shannon winds towards the place through an unadorned plain, approaching the striking magnificence of the sanctified spread of church-ruin, cross and tower placed along gentle tiered slopes. A rushy inlet further derogates the river as the final bend is manipulated and the full centre-stage is given to Clonmacnoise.

This County Offaly monastic site which so impressed Pope John Paul II lies a few miles north of Shannonbridge. Hundreds of tombstones, seven churches, three High Crosses, two holy wells and two round towers — an unparalleled archaeological *mise-en-scene*.

> In a quiet water'd land, a land of roses,
>   Stands Saint Kieran's city fair;
> And the warriors of Erin in their famous generations
>   Slumber there.
>
> There beneath the dewy hillside sleep the nobles
>   Of the clan of Conn,
> Each below his stone with name in branching Ogham
>   And the sacred knot thereon.
>
> There they laid to rest the seven Kings of Tara,
>   There the sons of Cairbré sleep –
> Battle-banners of the Gael that in Kieran's plain of crosses
> Now their final hosting keep.
>
> And in Clonmacnoise they laid the men of Teffia,
>   And right many a lord of Breagh;
> Deep the sod above Clan Creidé and Clan Conaill,
>   Kind in hall and fierce in fray.

Many and many a son of Conn, the Hundred-Fighter
  In the red earth lies at rest;
Many a blue eye of Clan Colman the turf covers,
  Many a swan-white breast.

It was from the Irish of Angus O'Gillan that Thomas William Rolleston of Shinrone translated the poem that eulogises a monastic city, a renowned craft and manuscript centre, a burial ground. In the sixth century lowly chariot maker's son, Ciaran, led eight companions from their Lough Ree monastery above Athlone. They sailed downstream and built a small wooden church at Clonmacnoise.

Tradition tells how Diarmuid, before becoming King of Tara, helped with the construction. He later lost his head – literally – while fighting in Ulster. The severed extremity was brought to Clonmacnoise for burial, thus perhaps establishing the place as a *capital* cemetery! It became customary for the remains of royalty and nobility to be brought to the great Shannonside ecclesiastical complex for their final repose. But as if to emphasise the inevitability of creative genius in a gifted race, the arts were thriving alongside the graves of leaders.

The *Book of the Dun Cow* (Leabhar na h-Uidre), the *Annals of Clonmacnoise* and of *Tigernach* are among the better known literary works that emanated from the cells of Ciaran's monks, while the Crozier of the Abbots of Clonmacnoise is a fine example of early Irish artistic craftsmanship.

The centre was plundered by the Vikings at least eight times. It was destroyed by fire up to thirteen times – once by the villain Turgesius who then allowed his wife Ota to perform druidic rites upon the main altar of the monastery.

In the Eaglais Beag (small church) or Teampall Ciaran, pilgrims scrape earth from a corner where once the patron's hand was kept as a relic.

A quaint piece of folklore concerns the round tower of Clonmacnoise which has had an unfinished appearance always. It reflects on the lack of generosity among its monks as much as upon the guile of the mason who built it.

When this craftsman was laying the final round of stones before commencing the topping-off, the clever clergy below removed the ladder, scaffolding, or whatever masons used in those days. Having the man at something of a disadvantage they began to dispute the price agreed upon for the building of the edifice. The mason, it could be said, was in a towering rage when the monks threatened that unless his price came down, he wouldn't.

But the crafty craftsman soon pulled himself together and nonchalantly

'Unfinished Round Tower' at Clonmacnoise

commenced taking down the tower and observing (for all the holy men to hear) that undoing his work was simple and that he would touch down within hours.

The monks became alarmed and asked the mason to parley, but he kept hurling down the stones. They then agreed to pay him the price asked, whereupon they erected the scaffolding for his descent. Down he came, demanded cash on the nail, took it and left Clonmacnoise vowing never to return to complete the work. Trade unions may have originated then, for the tower was 'blacked' and no mason would ever agree to complete it.

The authors who have written in praise of Clonmacnoise are outnumbered only by its own staggering total of archaeological wonders, all demanding the attention of chroniclers.

William Bulfin, born in Derrinlough near Birr in 1864, emigrated to Argentina in 1884 to work on the Pampas for four years before becoming a newspaper editor in Buenos Aires. An outspoken champion of Irish-Americans, he returned to this country, travelled its four provinces on a bicycle and wrote *Rambles in Erin,* a fascinating description of his tour. His account of a visit to Clonmacnoise is chosen for quotation because he best captures the mystique of its mélange of legend, history, fact and fiction. His narrative also evokes a fine Irish custom frequently observed at many of Shannon's holy places – the celebration of a pattern day.

'On all the roads between Banagher and Athlone there are troops of people facing westward. They are on vehicles of every kind, from the dashing excursion brake to the humble donkey cart, and every kind of bicycle procurable is also in evidence. Hundreds of people are tramping the roads in the dust; hundreds are footing it over the fields and hills; and there are many boats on the Shannon, all laden to the very gunwales with people from Connacht. And whether the crowds come out of Westmeath or Western Offaly, or from Galway or Roscommon, they are all converging in some common demomination; they are all on the way to Clonmacnoise of the Seven Churches. For this is the Sunday morning nearest to the 9th of September, the feast of St Ciaran (or Kieran). It is "pattern" or patron day – a day of prayer, or penance, and cheery festivity, too, and courtship and laughing and dancing – a day made up of Irish faith and Irish history, revealed in the softer lights of Irish character. I am going to the "pattern" myself, and I am taking the reader with me, if there is no objection.

'Two round towers, a wilderness of crumbling walls and naked gables, a forest of tombstones, and the wide river flowing peacefully through the callows which are studded with haycocks up to the very boundary of the cemetery. This is Clonmacnoise as we first catch sight of it from the Clogher road.

'There is a very long, low range of grassy hills between the bog and the river, and on the western slope of this ridge, just where the Shannon makes one of its magnificent loops, St Ciaran founded his little oratory on the 23rd of January A.D. 544. Ciaran died a few months afterward, but his oratory – the Eclais Beg – developed into a great seat of piety and learning, was surrounded in course of time by a populous city, and its name spread throughout Europe, from nearly every country of which scholars flocked to its schools and university.

'This holy place which we are approaching by the hilly roads that wind past the farmsteads of Clonfanlough is in ruins, for it has seen stormy times and it is very old. It was old before the Saracens were smashed at Tours, before Norman William landed at Hastings, before the Crusades were preached or fought. It was old before many of the present great universities of Christendom were founded, and before any of the present royal families of Europe were heard of in authentic history. It was old when the Danes raided its cloisters. It had celebrated the eleven hundredth anniversary of its foundation before the sacrilegious soldiery of Elizabeth reduced it to ruin. It flourished in the golden age of Christian Erin, and it received and holds the mortal remains of the last of the Irish Kings. All this is down in history; and it is written on the grey walls and tombs and monuments of the Seven Churches here beside the Shannon.

'Let us enter the ruins. Tread lightly on the graves which crowd the sward, for some of the noblest and loveliest and purest and greatest that Ireland has seen are sleeping here. This thought is assuredly present in the minds of those men and women who are praying in groups here and there. See, they have taken off their boots and stockings, and are going barefoot over the holy ground. They go round the graves of the saints on their knees. They kiss the floors of the churches. They tell their beads below the great sculptured cross in front of the Dananlaig or Tempull McDermott. They go bareheaded along the causeway to the old nunnery of Devorgilla. They cross themselves before drinking from the blessed wells. They whisper pious invocations as they drop hairpins or buttons or matches or pebbles into the niches and cavities where toothaches, headaches, warts and other ills are left behind.

'Here you have a husband and wife from beyond the Shannon who have come fasting for miles to "do the stations" and perform all the traditional devotions of the day. They are bareheaded, and their feet are bare and red from the scratches of briars and the stings of nettles. They are kneeling on the damp grass in front of the small cross now, and the man is giving out the Lord's Prayer in Irish. . .

'The word Clonmacnoise, according to John O'Mahony's note on page 94

View from Cathedral Window

of his translation of Keating, comes from Cluain-MacNois, signifying "the retreat of the sons of the noble", either from the great number of the sons of the Irish nobility who resorted to its college for education, or from many of the Irish princes having burial places in its cemetery. Joyce says it means "the meadow of the Son of Nos". *The Four Masters* call it by the same name practically. St Ciaran took only four months to build his Eclais Beg. The following legend regarding the founding of Clonmacnoise is told in the "Chronicon Scotrum", and also in the "Leabhar Buidhe Lecain".

'When Ciaran was planting the first post to mark out the ground at Clonmacnoise, Diarmuid Mac Cearbhaill, a young prince who was a fugitive in the district, helped the Saint with his own hands to drive the pole into the ground. "Though your companions today are few," said Ciaran, "tomorrow thou shalt be High King of Erin." One of Diarmuid's companions was Maelmor, his foster brother, and, hearing the prophecy, this man went and slew King Tauthal Maelgarbh, great grandson of Niall the Great, who had set a price on Diarmuid's head. The men from Tara and Meath then sought out Diarmuid, who was the true heir to the Ardrighship, and proclaimed him High King of Erin. On the Great Cross in front of Tempull McDermott the saint and the King are represented on one of the sculptured panels with their hands on a pole in commemoration of the founding of Clonmacnoise.

'Diarmuid ascended the throne of Tara in A.D. 544. It was during his reign that Tara was cursed by St Ruadhan of Lorrha. Soon after the curse was pronounced Tara was deserted. . .

'Here is the ruin known as "Devorgilla's Nunnery". She was the wife of Tiernan O'Rourke of Breffney who eloped with MacMorrough. She repented of her sin and separated from her paramour after two years. . . to spend the rest of her life doing good works. This is one of the convents she built. The doorway of the chapel is still beautiful. It was repaired some years ago. It is of the flat-arched Norman school, which would in time have developed into a style distinctly Irish. Even as it is there is a distinctiveness about it which is worthy of close study. It marks undoubtedly the beginning of a school of architectural design which had many splendid possibilities.

'Have you noticed how Clonmacnoise brackets two Irish names fraught with tragic significance – Diarmuid and Devorgilla? Diarmuid lived centuries before Devorgilla, and was of character quite different to that of the faithless wife of Drumahaire. But connected with each of their names, although for widely different reasons, there is a chapter of history crowded with the ruin of Ireland.

'There are tents beside the narrow road leading from the cemetery to the highway. There are apple carts, ginger bread carts, shooting galleries, and

Carvings representing St Dominic, St Patrick and St Francis above the cathedral doorway

other enterprises, sporting and commercial. We make our way through them and gain the open fields beside the Shannon. The day has flown quickly, and the feast is over now.'

Over too is William Bulfin's account which differs from those of eminent historians and archaeologists in some aspects of chronology and spelling. But accuracy of date and of letter is of little consequence in so fascinating a narrative by one of Offaly's rarest sons. It does not merely capture the true atmosphere of a very sacred place on pattern day. Its nomadic prose is sympathetic to the very subject of this book in its air of timelessness, in its antique style, in its elegant simplicity.

Shannonbridge

The Ballinasloe-Cloughan road crosses the Shannon at Shannonbridge, and the Connaught bridgehead was secured by a fort built in the early nineteenth century. To a person passing down the one-street village, the Shannon Navigation Office is striking in its quaintness but the bridge beyond is narrow. Viewed from the river, however, the structure is imposing with its sixteen fine arches.

One bombardier and six gunners of the Royal Artillery manned the permanent magazine situated there in 1804. In that year too, Lt Colonel Henry Hutton inspected all the Shannon defensive field-works and reported on the number and type of armament at Shannonbridge, Athlone, Banagher, Keelogue and Meelick. Shannonbridge boasted seven twelve-pounders and three howitzers (8") in field-works, together with another seven twelve-pounders and one eight-inch howitzer at the Batteries.

Field-work were temporary gun-emplacements dug into the earth and heightened by the soil taken out, supported by wooden palisades. Permanent fortifications were developed and the troops used for their construction were billeted in the village. The building was on the south side of the street and was used as a Garda barracks until the mid-1970s.

The final bridgehead defences at Shannonbridge were built of squared rubble as was its barracks. The defences were thought to be unique in Western Europe. *The Parliamentary Gazetteer of Ireland* said, in 1844: '. . . The Roscommon end of the bridge is occupied by a military work, which forms a *tête-du-pont* capable of accommodating a small garrison. The public road wends between barracks and fort passing through a strong gate; the place besides being defended by the guns of the fort is protected on the Connaught side by an advance redoubt on rising ground north of the highway. . . Shannonbridge is one of the three fortified passes still maintained upon the Shannon, the other two being Banagher and Athlone. . .'

Preserved as they are by the Office of Public Works, the Shannonbridge defences show how Humbert's landing in 1798 left the British authorities in trepidation, causing the expenditure of large sums of money in preparation for a possible Napoleonic invasion from the western seaboard.

This concern with things military puts in mind the fact that a composer of rousing marching lyrics spent some of his early years in Shannonbridge. His best known poem – the music which became the signature tune of Radio Éireann in its march form – is 'O'Donnell Aboo!' Michael Joseph McCann died in 1833 in the capital city of the Saxon whom many of his poems decried. His lesser-known ballad of the Pale called 'The Battle of Glenmalure,' has verses that are in accord with a departure from a slumbering riverside village with a soldiering tradition – of a difference!

And now, above the rugged glen, their prancing steeds they rein,
While many an eager look along its mazy depths they strain,
But where's the martialled foe they seek – the camp or watch fires – where?
For save the eagle screaming high, no sign of life is there!

I've heard it is the traitor's wont in cave and swamp to hide
When e'er they deem their force too weak the battle's brunt to bide;
So, mark! Where'er a rebel lurks, arouse him in his lair –
And death to him whose hand is known an Irish foe to spare.

Shannon Harbour

Meeting the Canal

Leitch Ritchie had some comment to make on the hotel at Shannon Harbour. He thought it a bit on the big side for such a place but: '. . . "The passengers by canal from Dublin are very numerous," reasoned the projector, "and of course we must have an hotel of proportionable size to receive them." He did not consider that there is nothing in Shannon Harbour to detain these passengers: who immediately on their arrival embark in the steamboat, where they are supplied not only with lodging but provisions, while all the time they are progressing on their journey. . .'

The canal boat company attempted to deliver customers to their destinations in a reasonably sober condition:

'FIRST CABIN. – Wine sold only in pints or half-pints – and not more than one pint to each person. A noggin of spirits, or half a noggin of spirits and a half a pint of wine, allowed to each gentleman after dinner or supper-time: such allowance of spirits not extended to ladies, or wine or spirits to children

76

River Steamers from early postcards

under ten years; nor is the allowance of wine or spirits of one person, without his or her express desire, to be transferred to another.'

But note well the liberated ladies of the lower class:

'SECOND CABIN. – No more than two bottles of porter, ale, or cider, or one bottle of any two of them, allowed to each male passenger, and one of any of them to each female, throughout the journey; and any passenger bringing liquor into the boat, and using it, to forfeit his passage.'

A nasty mind might read the most alarming implications into that final instruction!

Not unduly complimentary to our liveried lady thus far, Mr Ritchie, did concede, moving downriver from Shannon Harbour: 'It is still indeed a swamp, but very beautiful. Everywhere islands appeared rising just to the line of the water, and displaying a surface hardly discernible from it, except by the hayricks which proved their fertility. By and by the islands were thickly clothed with wood; and as the vessel wound between them in narrow and intricate passages, I might have imagined myself in the wilds of the new world. The trees appeared to spring from the deep, for the low banks were completely submerged. Before, behind and around us were these floating lumps of foliage; and vistas opened here and there by our side, showing other islands and a further expanse of deep and tranquil water. I do not know that, in viewing natural scenery, I have ever felt emotions more new, and more delightful. The romantic associations that are suspended while the world is present, came back upon my heart, and I felt that I was enjoying the reality of a dream. . .'

Irish River Floatels- "St. James", "St. Patrick" and "Linquenda"

Floatels from early postcards

River Steamer from an early postcard

Banagher to Portumna

RICHARD HARVEY wrote of Banagher: 'The town was incorporated by charter of 4th Charles I. The corporation was called "The Sovereign, Burgesses, and Free Commons of the borough and town of Bannacher, *alias* Bannagher"; and possessed and exercised the power of sending two members to Parliament. At the date of the Union, however, the Right Hon. William Brabazon Ponsonby carried the borough in his pocket, wielded all its powers, and received the whole £15,000 of compensation for the loss of its franchise. . .

'In the immediate neighbourhood of the town are the ruins of Garry Castle, a fortalice of the MacColgans, chiefs of the district, who built a strong castle here, which was surrendered to Ireton in the Parliamentary war; the last male representative of this family, Thomas Colgan Esq. M.P. for the borough of Banagher, died in 1790. The last of the family must be considered as the last of the Irish chieftains. . .'

The Second Report of the Commissioners for the Improvement of the River Shannon commented, in 1837: 'Banagher, where we also propose that a new bridge should be erected, is. . . an important communication across the river, though not so generally useful as Athlone; it is situated between the county of Galway, and the King's County, and we are of the opinion that the moiety of the expense of its erection should be made up equally between these counties. . .'

79

The moiety was £25,000 and the bridge was built between 1841 and 1843.

Several famous writers spent some time in Banagher. Anthony Trollope, the English novelist wrote two books set in Shannon's hinterland. He was a Post Office Surveyor's Clerk – and not a very good one, for he arrived in Ireland in 1851 with a rather ragged record. He was promoted to Inspector of Postal Deliveries and part of his job was the investigation of complaints, of which he said there were few. He submitted reports on defaulting postmasters too.

Part of his service was spent in Banagher: 'I was to live at a place called Banagher on the Shannon which I had heard of because of its having once been conquered, though it had heretofore conquered everything, including the devil.'

Trollope liked the place and the people: 'I soon found them to be good humoured, clever – the working classes much more intelligent than those of England – economical and hospitable. We hear much of their spendthrift nature, but extravagance is not the nature of an Irishman. He will count the shillings in a pound much more accurately than an Englishman and will with much more certainty get twelve penny worth for each.'

The Bank of Ireland building in Banagher, built circa 1875, retains its dignified original lines

'That beats Banagher' must have been Trollope's cry when he investigated a written complaint upriver in Drumsna. It was with great trepidation that he approached the house of the complainant, his language in the letter not having been very complimentary to post office officials. He need not have worried for he was taken in, wined, dined and slept before the business in hand was discussed. 'Oh that!' said the Drumsna dissenter. 'Forget about it. The postal service is not too bad; I just love to write letters.'

The Shannonsiders became a trifle cool towards the Englishman, however, when he married an Englishwoman: 'I had given offence and I was made to feel it.'

Perhaps this was partly because this Shannonside town was noted for its industrious maidens who were particulaly adept at spinning. The town attracted wayfaring bachelors from far afield who came in search of a good wife:

> If you fancy a one that's a bundle of fun
> Have a look in Drumsna or Keadue;
> If it's one without looks but who spins and who cooks –
> Then Banagher town is for you.

Charlotte Bronte, whose best known works were *Villette, The Professor* and *Jane Eyre,* did not like Banagher. Her father, Rev. Patrick from County Down, was the son of Hugh Prunty. He taught school in Drumgooland before changing his name and leaving to study in Cambridge. He became a Church of England clergyman and brought up his talented daughters Charlotte, Emily Jane and Anne in a secluded Yorkshire parsonage. His curate, Rev. Arthur Bell-Nicholls married Charlotte in 1854 and part of their honeymoon was spent in Banagher.

At the Royal School in Banagher the head of a remarkable literary family studied. Sir William Wilde, eye-surgeon, antiquarian and medical commissioner for the Irish census, wrote on travel and on Irish folkways and superstitions. He loved to quote the gentle May-Day song:

> Samhradh, Samhradh, bainne na ngamhna
> Thugamar féin an samhradh linn,
> An samhradh buí 'san nóinín gléigeal
> Is thugamar féin an samhradh linn.

Having witnessed the funeral of Thomas Davis at the age of nineteen, Wilde's wife became an ardent nationalist. Under the pseudonym Speranza

81

she wrote for *The Nation*. She too wrote of folklife. The couple had a son who is not unknown. His name was Oscar!

Not far from the Galway bank of Shannon, near Banagher, is the small town of Eyrecourt, named after a Cromwellian family. George Eyre, a late eighteenth century M.P., was a master of the famous Galway Blazers, a hunt whose members had tendencies towards arson. While visiting Birr in County Offaly they burned down the inn where they celebrated – Dooley's Hotel.

Eyrecourt has many tales of gallous deeds, many songs and ballads of events concerned with outwitting 'the gentry'. It has one of Ireland's many crocks of gold, said to be hidden beneath the flagstones of its endowed school. No leprechaun guards this academic trove, but rather the ghost of a Protestant clergyman, the Rev. Mr Banks. This gentleman was said to have possessed the largest pair of *glaums*(hands) in the land. 'You could shovel sand with them and mix the mortar with the thumb,' remarked a Shannon boatman from Clonfert.

Residents of the area convenient to the school were nervous of the ministerial meanderings, manual magnificence and morbid manifestations of the late cleric. A very frightened bachelor awoke one night as a November moon stole through a crack in the shutter, throwing a weak light across the foot of his bed. The horrified man was sure that he saw a huge pair of hands reaching above the ends of his blankets. He dived for his gun which he kept nearby for such emergencies. He aimed, fired twice in quick succession – and shot his own feet off.

A drunken Eyrecourt man saw what he described as 'a big black thing with horns' outside the school one night. Fortified to accomplish deeds of great valour by the black liquid welling within, he challenged the apparition:

> If you're a living person, go home,
> If you're a spirit, go to heaven,
> And if you're a divil – go to hell.

Eyrecourt was a popular drinking spot for bargees stopping at Shannon Harbour. They came from all over; many were from Offaly and Galway, some from County Kildare and Dublin city. They were big hefty men with not only a witty turn of phrase in plain English but also a language or cant of their own, too complicated for a landlubber or even ordinary river boatmen to understand. A man who owned a barge was called a *hackman*. A blind hackman once had two sons. One was thin and so nicknamed Shinny (skinny); the other stout one was called Hoggy. The blind hackman would lean on his tiller knowing that Shinny was on the rope-side and Hoggy on the skuttle-side. (The skuttle was the entrance to the barge.) The litany would be heard on a calm evening: 'Up to Shinny. Over to Hoggy. Back to Shinny. Across to Hoggy.' Thereafter, port or rope-side was always *shinny* and starboard or skuttle-side *hoggy.*

They were amusing too in English. After the Civil War one bargee who plied the Grand Canal walked ever after with a slight limp and boasted: 'I'm carrying lead for Ireland, got in a naval encounter.' He had been fired on from the bank by someone with a shotgun!

Another time a man carrying on a petty smuggling racket inquired if he would be safe trying to get through Eyrecourt quietly. He didn't appreciate the reply: 'A wind would have a better chance of sneaking past a poplar tree.'

But lest the good people of Eyrecourt and district be offended at being singled out for levity, an assurance must be given that, like all people with life and humour, they are the salt of the earth. As they would say, 'You can write it down they are.'

> O'er the rath of Mullaghmast
> On the solemn midnight blast
> What bleeding spectres passed,
> With their gashed breasts bare?
> Hast thou heard the fitful wail
> That o'erloads the sullen gale,
> When the waning moon shines pale
> O'er the curst ground there?

It might well be asked what place has the poem of Richard Dalton Williams, describing a County Kildare slaughter, in a book about Shannon? The answer lies in a fascinating piece of legend concerning Meelick Abbey below Bangher.

'Shamrock' of *The Nation* wrote the poem to commemorate an event that took place in 1577. The heads of Laois and Offaly clans and other chieftains were invited to a soirée near Ballitore. On the guest list was one Donal O' Madden, Lord of Siol Anmchadha. He accepted the invitation of the English in good faith and set out with his heir, Ambrose, to meet escorts at Lusmagh, the O'Madden stronghold on the Shannon's east bank. These escorts were to accompany him to Mullaghmast.

As the pair approached Meelick the bell of Vespers tolled from the Abbey and both tarried a while to pray. They had just resumed their journey when Ambrose's horse shied and became very agitated, its mane stood on its neck and it reared up on its hind legs. Then gradually it became calm but refused to move another pace forward.

Then there appeared the phantom of a long-lost warrior of the O'Madden clan. This spectre warned the pair of the plan to massacre all the guests at Mullaghmast. Donal and Ambrose returned to their homes and thus escaped almost certain death, for only one chieftain, an O'Moore, is alleged to have escaped from that neat English trap.

Meelick Abbey was founded in 1414, built by Eoghan O'Madden for the Franciscan friars. Fergus O'Madden is buried there. As Lord of Siol Anmchadha, O'Madden was in line for the High Kingship of Ireland when his bard, O'Dugain, composed a great poem which lauded his master's triumphs and attributes while subtly hinting at the nobility of his lineage. He advised Eoghan not to seek or accept High Kingship but to aim at becoming Prince of Uí Maine, thereby following the tradition of seven others of his sept. He further urged Eoghan never to give up the 'Flowery Plain of Meelick'

> Nor the angelic Oran
> Nor lovely Lough Greine
> Of the bright salmons;
> Nor the Mountains of Sliabh Murray
> Of the smooth grass;
> Nor the winding ways
> Of Lordly Shannon.

During the Elizabethan invasion, the O'Madden stronghold at Lusmagh resisted siege for nineteen years but eventually was stormed and taken. Almost 200 O'Maddens were put to the sword by Sir William Russell, the Lord Deputy, and were flung over the battlements to add more Irish blood to Shannon's waters. Meelick's stronghold thus was lost and the abbey was pillaged. It fell into decay thereafter and remained derelict until 1686.

The friars were forced to leave yet again during the Williamite rebellion, but not for long. The abbey's doors were never again closed until the Famine when near-starvation within its community forced a cessation of hospitality. It was then that another Madden, Richard Robert, historian of the United Irishmen, visited Meelick. Moved by its depression he wrote:

> The solemn chant is heard no more,
> Within that venerable pile;
> The Vesper hymn that softly bore
> The Virgin's praise from aisle to aisle.

The sounds, the sights that gave a soul
To piety no more are there,
No more absorb each sense, control
Each thought and wrap the mind in prayer.

Portumna

A velvet-bound, gilt-edged volume entitled *Ireland, Picturesque and Romantic* by Leitch Ritchie includes the passage: 'The young girl before us, although her action is not boisterous, is dancing with soul and body. Her eyes, feet and hair jig at the same moment. Her hair, indeed is rather out of bounds in its amusement, considering that is was actually combed in the morning – a discipline of extraordinary rarity. But this is the consequence of habit, and may easily be forgiven, especially on a fair day. . . She. . . is Spanish all over, with a dash of indolent voluptuousness which proclaims her ancestry. If she belonged to the country farther north, her face would have been round instead of oval, her eyes small, and her nose short, sharp and retroussé. If farther north still, she would have rejoiced in the strongly-marked and somewhat rigid features of the Scots. . .'

The aforegoing description, written early in the nineteenth century, was of a Portumna girl performing an Irish jig. This physiognomic observation was in harmony with the theory that a Spanish colony in Galway spread itself but never crossed the Shannon.

Portumna Castle, completed in 1618, was built by Richard de Burgh, the Earl of Clanricarde. Formerly belonging to the O'Maddens (of whom more was heard up-river at Meelick), the Portumna estates passed in the sixteenth century to the Clanricarde Burkes (or de Burghs or de Burgos).

By any name, Clanricarde's Earls were not always true. During the reign of Elizabeth I one of them watched his son being executed for not ridding Connaught of rebels.

A story is told of another de Burgo who befriended a certain Cormac Roe O'Moore during their youth. Each swore to assist the other throughout the tribulations of their lives ahead.

Many years later, as a result of the perpetual warfare between the Irish chieftains and their English oppressors, Cormac found himself being pursued through Clanricarde's estates near Portumna. He remembered their promises of boyhood and decided to contact de Burgo at his keep on Wren's Island in the Shannon. But the blackguard de Burgo heard of Cormac's coming and removed all his boats from the Connaught side of the river so that he could not be reached by O'Moore or his men.

Possessed by a great anger, Cormac called on his men to ride their horses

Portumna Castle gates

into the river and kill them before the pursuing English arrived. They did this and he then commanded them to tie the beasts together forming a pontoon of horseflesh across which to march to Wren's Island. They wiped out de Burgo's men and Cormac slew his former friend for his inhospitable action:

> For now along the farther shore,
> The English host was seen,
> Whilst Erin's sons 'gainst Erin's sons
> Plied sabre, pike and skein.

Gortachaha means the field of the battle and that spot has its place in ancient verse:

> Lone is the spot and oft' forgot
> Though once well known and famed;
> Yet to this day, since that dread fray,
> 'Tis Gortachaha names.

The last Earl of Clanricarde was said to have been the meanest man in Ireland. He was feeding one of his tenant workers one day. On the plate he placed a large heap of turnips and a tiny helping of beef. It was said that 'You'd see more flesh on a tinker's stick after a fair in Mullingar.' The plate was soon clean and the Earl inquired if his tenant wanted more.

'Another tiny piece of beef,' asked the man.

He received another miserable portion – but with plenty of turnips.

He finished that plateful and the same thing happened. Large helpings of turnips and tiny pieces of beef were the order of the day until eventually the Earl said, 'God, but you're an awful hungry man, Dan. It's how you'll have a bullock in your stomach.'

'Well if I have,' said Dan, 'it won't be roarin' for turnips, that's for sure.'

The warring clans of Connaught are the subject of a song that has a proud reputation for saving Irish ceilís, sing-songs and parties from flagging. Its lyrics are by Thomas Davis, its air stirring and vibrant. And if it fails to rouse malingering roisterers to vocal involvement, it will at least begin a good argument for its title has been given as *The West's Asleep* and *The West's Awake*. Its third verse is quoted here:

For often in O'Connor's van,
To triumph dashed each Connaught clan,
And fleet as deer the Normans ran
Thro' Corrsliabh Pass and Ardrahan;
And later times saw deeds as brave,
And glory guards Clanricarde's grave,
Sing, Oh! they died their lands to save
At Aughrim's slopes and Shannon's wave.

Lough Derg

NO BOOK dwelling on the Shannon's literature would be complete if it did not allude to Terryglass, seven miles from Portumna on the Tipperary shore of Lough Derg. Buried there, tradition claims, is Flann Mac Lonan — one of the three principal poets of Connaught and *ollamh* of Ireland up to his murder in 893. Called the 'Devil's Son' because of his satirical verse, traditionally he is regarded as the earliest professional Irish poet. With Finglas and Tallaght, Terryglass was regarded as a great seat of learning and it survived until the middle of the twelfth century.

This connection with Leinster is significant, for the original monastery was founded by St Colman (one of the dozen disciples of Clonard's celebrated St Finian) in the mid-sixth century. Around the turn of the thirteenth century the *Leabhar na Nuachongbhala,* later known as the *Book of Leinster* was commissioned by Kildare's Bishop Finn. This work, said to sum up 'all the learning of the monastic period of Irish writing' was worked upon at Terryglass by Aed Ua Cremthainn, a scholar of the court of 'the High King of the Southern Half of Ireland'.

Very little remains of early or medieval origin here. Shameful neglect of an eminent site angers, and its vacuous stare demands verbal condemnations:

> Tí-da-glas —
> Land of the twin streams —
> Lapped by the Red Lake's salve;
> Nature's condolence
> For man's neglect.
> Colman, Columba, Aed
> Trod here.

Great seat of learning
And of piety,
Locked in a spoorless night
Of oblivion.

Terryglass has been snatched for special mention before committing the finest lake on the Shannon to the superficial treatment demanded by the limits of publishing. Lough Derg could well be the subject of a substantial tome and no shorter work could do justice to her wealth of history, of beauty, of lore.

The lake's virtues are as plentiful as the authors who attempted to enumerate or describe them. Every tree on every bank, every stone of every island, every fold in every inlet holds a story, a fable, a fact of history. It is as if the Shannon, sensing that her meeting with the sea was imminent, took one final and mighty heave by which she would expand to embrace as much as possible of the countryside. This great indulgement in the visual and intellectual attractions of Clare and Galway on her west bank and Tipperary on her east, constitutes a metaphysical fusion that fires an aspiration close to hedonism in the mind of the observer.

The *Parliamentary Gazetteer of Ireland* for 1844-45 gave the clinical details:

'DERG, the lowest, the longest, and greatly the most picturesque of the expansions of the river Shannon. It extends from north-north-east to south-south-west. . . Its length is 23 English miles; and its breadth varies between 2 and 6 English miles.

'At its head is Portumna; at its foot is Killaloe; near its west shores are Woodford, Mount-Shannon, and Scariff; and near its east shores are Borris-o-kane and Nenagh. Two large bays project from its west side towards Dorus and Scariff; and five considerable bays project toward Borris, Nenagh and other places on the east. Numerous rivulets enter each side; and, in several instances, are remarkable for either their greatness of volume, or their subserviency to navigation. Isles and islets are profusely sprinkled over most parts, particularly Scariff bay, and the great reach thence to Portumna; several of these possess interest for either their harbours or their ancient monuments; and most combine with the surrounding waters and shores to produce a series of effective landscapes. The upper part of the lake. . . is tame and even insipid; more than one half of the eastern shore, from the head downwards, rarely rises above the softly and ornately beautiful; but all the remainder is magnificent – screened by lofty and variform hills, and possessing many of the elements of lacustrine grandeur. So naturally free is the whole lake for navigation, that the Commissioners for Improving the Navigation of the

Fishing on Lough Derg

Islands on Lough Derg, from the Tipperary side

90

Shannon proposed to spend upon it only about £300. . .'

The *Gazatteer* continues to give, in acres roods and perches, the area of the lake itself and of its allotment to counties and parishes.

In his *Journey throughout Ireland during the Spring, Summer, and Autumn of 1834*, Henry D. Inglis incorporated the inevitable tourist comment on the Irish weather which takes from the claims that our summers of yester-year were long lazy days of sunshine: 'I stepped on board the steam vessel at eight in the morning, satisfied with everything about Killaloe, excepting the inn, which is far from being what might be expected at the place where the Navigation Company has fixed its headquarters. About a mile and a half from Killaloe, just at the entrance to Lough Derg, is a mount on the left bank covered with trees, where it is said the ancient kings once resided. On entering Lough Derg, several pretty and interesting objects attract one on both sides. The vessel kept nearly mid-water, and the first reach of the lough being only about a mile wide, there is nothing lost to the eye. Derry Castle, the residence of Captain Head, on the Tipperary side, is a beautiful spot: the lawn slopes down to the water; the house is almost hidden in fine woods; and there is a fine background of cultivated mountains. On a little island, close to the shore, are seen the ruins of a castle.

'All the way through this first reach of the lough, a distance of about four miles, the character of the bank continues the same: not that there is anything like monotony; all the variety that can be produced by verdure, wood, and tillage, is there: but the banks are invariably sloping and cultivated, with higher and more sterile elevations rising behind; ten or twelve islands, of inconsiderable size, lie scattered over this first reach. At the point where this first reach of the loch terminates, opening into the wider part of the lake, the banks on both sides are extremely beautiful. The Clare side is covered with deep woods, backed by lofty hills; and the Tipperary side is adorned by the fine domain of Castle-lough, embosomed in magnificent oak woods: here, too, an island surmounted by a ruin, is seen on the right, close to the shore; and a small harbour has been constructed in a little bay, for the convenience of the export of slate. This first reach of the lough varies in depth from thirty up to ninety feet; but in the mid-channel, the average depth is from seventy to eighty feet. Close to the shore, there is generally from ten to fifteen feet of water; and at some parts as much as forty feet.

'Immediately on emerging from the first reach, the lough spreads both to the left and right. The left reach. . . is an interesting one. . . On the Clare side, the nearer banks are finely cultivated and well wooded; and more than one ruined castle is seen rising from the water's edge. One of these castles was some time ago held in forcible possession by illicit distillers, against all the

91

Mount Shannon, Co. Clare

civil force that attempted, from time to time, to dislodge them: and it was at length found necessary to batter down the sheltering walls with cannon ball. On the Galway side, the scenery is diversified by several fine country seats, and by the prettily situated village of Mount-Shannon.

'Several islands, also, adorn this reach; particularly Holy Island, covered with beautiful green pasturage, on which there is an extensive grazing; and where also is one of the ancient Round Towers, besides some lesser and more imperfect ruins. The other islands are no way remarkable. With the exception of Bushy island, which is what it professes to be, they are destitute of wood.

'Leaving this reach. . . we now turn into the main reach of the lough. The banks are now, for a few miles less interesting on the Tipperary side; but on the Galway shore, several gentlemen's seats are seen. . .

'. . . The slow rate at which the steamer carried us through the lake afforded ample time for observation; and although the weather was not what would generally be called fine, and gave rise to much grumbling among the passengers, I was not among the number of grumblers. It was not, indeed, one of those splendid summer days, when lakes are like mirrors, and woods are mirrored in them; when the green slopes seem to bask in sunshine, and repose dwells among the hills. It was all sorts of weather: we had gleams of sunshine; sudden mists; flying showers; moments of calm; sweeping breezes. . .

92

'After passing Cow island, the lough bends a little to the left; and just at the bend, we passed close to an island called Flanmore (Illaunmore).. . on the Tipperary shore, villas are scattered here and there. . . The domain of Castle Biggs is particularly attractive. . . on the Galway side, the banks are thickly covered with wood, which is not however of large growth; and a wild uninteresting tract of country reaches along Cloongaggave Bay – the last into which the lough expands on the left. . .'

That less than enthusiastic account of a trip up Lough Derg by a London visitor does expose the keen eye of the stranger for fine houses, good seats and villas in the midst of nature's most artistic panorama.

An Oxonian, S. Reynolds Hole, Dean of Rochester, also made *A Little Tour of Ireland* in the mid-nineteenth century. He had passed Clonmacnoise and called it the Eton of Ireland 'by whom despoiled and desecrated we English need not pause to inquire. . .' He dismissed Lough Derg in two lines, one of which was 'There are delightful residences on either side. . .' His work reeks of *och hones* and assorted banalities. Five pages are devoted to a parody on the *Bells of Shandon,* the quality of which may be judged by the following excerpt:

> With maid and man on,
> A steamer ran on,
> Where silver Shannon
> In glory glames!
> Shure, all big rivers
> He bates to shivers,
> Rowling majestic,
> This King o' Strames!

Dromineer, Puckaun, Garrykennedy, Bellevue facing Meelick, Mountshannon, Tintrim, Rinbarra – why their very names give Derg a dignity. If less than adequate writings have been chosen on behalf of her peerless waters and surrounds, it is in the confident knowledge that she speaks for herself – in the whisper of soft breezes through her arboreal collar, in the chuckle of her fleece-capped eddies, in the echoes of a distinguished past sounding across her waters.

To Killaloe and Beyond

LET US NOW pick up the story of the kindly writer we last met at Clonmacnoise as he travels on his bicycle towards the base of the lough. Here is how William Bulfin describes a stretch of Shannon:

'I turned westward in Nenagh, and picked up the Shannon once more at Portroe, where Lough Derg narrows into a long strip of water, not more than a mile in width, bordered on the Clare side by the wooded hills which rise into the Bernagh range. The Tipperary side is relatively flat, but very picturesque; and from this point to Killaloe the Shannon is indeed lordly. But it is, unfortunately, an empty, profitless lordship. It is not the lordship of the Rhine or the Rhone or the Danube. It is devoid of the traffic of commerce. The magnificent river is not a factor in the national economy. Its potentialities are asleep. The Shannon is mighty, but idle.

'There is a little island in Lough Derg, opposite Portroe, which has a very ancient and illustrious history. It is small in area, not more than two score acres more or less, but in the early days of the Church in Ireland it was the site

Ruins of St Caimin's Church, Iniscaltra

of one of the great schools of Thomond. The island is called Iniscaltra, and the seat of learning of which it was the home was one of the greatest schools in Ireland during the seventh and eighth centuries. The school was founded by St Columba, of Terryglass. He died in 552. Another great man, and more famous scholar than St Columba, ruled in Iniscaltra a hundred years later. His name was Caimin. Iniscaltra is deserted and silent now; and the tall round tower merely calls attention to the spot where once stood the church and schools. There is not a word of all this in the guide books. Nine out of every ten tourists who pass it on the Shannon pleasure steamers give it but a careless glance, and think no more about it. Only a round tower — another of them — and a few crumbling walls, and nothing more but green, green rich grass and Galway cattle. Yet there was a time when scholars came hither from many lands. A scion of the Lagenian race and a descendant of a Leinster King was its rector. He was the trusted friend of St Finian of Clonard, and one whose word went far in the councils of the sages and scholars of Erin.

'The road turns southward, now running close to the waterside, through scenery which it would be hard to surpass in beauty even in Ireland. You have to loiter here and there and fill your eyes with pictures of the blue water and the green fields and the noble woods — all to be retained in the memory and carried away. There is scarcely a sound, only the soft voice of the wavelets on the shore, and the splash of a fish leaping after a fly, and the low song of the trees. But this soft harmony is ripped open by the grating hen-like note of a pheasant in a whin clump under the pines, and through the slit in the pulsating silence come far-off voices over the water, from a sail boat gliding leisurely down stream. I am encamped in a tangle of grass and bracken, with the tuneful woods above me and the Shannon spread out below, and I find it very fresh and sweet and restful.'

The Shannon's secrets come to light in the most unlikely places. At Killaloe Cathedral, copperplate writing in a copious bound volume labelled BAPTISMS MARRIAGES AND BURIALS. *Registers for Killaloe Parish,* tells the details of seventeenth century Claremen initiated, imprisoned and interred. Among these entries, the following appears: 'Extract from old Vestry Book of Killaloe Cathedral The 30th July 1698. A great winde wch. broak & burned trees & every sort of thing & wth. all druve back & stopped ye river Shanan from running its natural course for ye space of 3 hours at Killalow so yat there were severall went and walked drye from in ye water course of ye said Shanan to the County of Tipperary yat by means thereof there was a bundance of fish taken in ye place thereof.'

That in itself is interesting, but then comes an insertion in different handwriting and darker ink, obviously an addendum of twenty-eight years

Killaloe Cathedral

Kilfenora Cross in Killaloe Cathedral

Ogham Stone in Killaloe Cathedral

96

later: 'And in the year 1726 on the same day of the same month & ye same day of the week bein Saturday hapned the same occurrence as above at Killaloe.'

The magnificent old St Flannan's Cathedral on Shannon's banks contains a honeysuckle ornamented Romanesque doorway, possibly the west door of a former edifice built by Donal Mór O'Brien. A Kilfenora Cross and the Ogham Stone nearby with its runic and ogham inscriptions make this an unique corner of historic interest. For some inexplicable reason, antiquities preserved in a place of worship seem to have an added significance. A veneration of heritage is implied as stillness paradoxically amplifies whispers from a past extolling Christianity, scholarship and peace. And from without, the hushed Shannon replies:

> A part of his Almighty power,
>   To profit man, God lent my tide;
> And here, along my winding shore
>   Millions of souls might be employ'd!
> From year to year my mighty flood
>   To ocean's caves is idly hurl'd,
> Whose strength would give an active soul
>   To the trade-engines of the world!
>
> The sordid few whose barren gold,
>   Could thus a nation's hands employ,
> Like greedy otters watch and war,
>   About my fish and timid fry!
> The cormorants that haunt my flood
>   Are less voracious for their prey,
> Than those insatiate human-sharks
>   That watch my current, night and day!
>
> God stored my stream with finny wealth,
>   And boundless is his bounty there
> From year to year 'tis well supplied,
>   For all his poor to have a share!
> But proud monopolists now claim,
>   And covet this great public right,
> And use a ruthless robber-law
>   To sanctify their lawless might!

There is no justice in the land
    Where *law* such evil work can do,
The right of thousands to convey
    Unto the greedy-gasping few!
But God permits the weak a time,
    Thus to be trampled by the strong;
Yet He has iron limits fixed
    To every course of human wrong.

The Shannon re-echoes the lament of her wheelwright Bard of Thomond. But quoted more than a century after its creation, the lust for her 'finny wealth' is but an analogy to illustrate the fierce universal greed and avarice that have beset the land. Heavy articulated trucks are said to be shaking the foundations of St Flannan's Cathedral. A cathedral's silent splendour being shattered — a cathedral's and a nation's.

Killaloe Bridge

Killaloe from the air

But the Shannon dwells not to mourn or to indict. Bidding farewell to Killaloe and Slieve Bernagh above her, she hurries ahead. According to Ritchie:

'The river from Killaloe to Limerick is among the finest things in Ireland. Here you have green and sloping banks – there islands like emeralds set in silver – beyond, magnificent woods that fling their shadow over the stream – and, finest of all, the rushing, roaring, foaming rapids of the Shannon. Within this trifling space there is every thing which, in natural scenery, can amuse, excite, soften, or astonish. . .'

Castleconnell, which gave its name to a salmon rod, once guarded the river's rapids, later spoiled by the Shannon Hydro-electric Scheme. Here Brian Boru's grandson was murdered. Here too the Earl of Desmond slew the son of William de Burg in 1578. Queen Elizabeth sympathised with William and created him Baron of Castleconnell with a yearly pension of 100 marks. The second baron, John Burke was in London in 1592, where he had a dispute with Captain Arnold Cosby. A duel was decided upon and John arrived on his

The Rapids at Castleconnell

Energy!

BREWSTER

90,000 HORSE POWER

Of energy will be available from the Shannon Electrical Power Station next year for Irish Industry and Irish homes.

The American workman is the most prosperous on earth, because he has, on an average, three horse-power, the equivalent of thirty human slaves, helping him to produce.

No wonder he can toil less and be paid more than the workman of other lands. He is not a toiler, he is a director of machinery.

Wages and prosperity are determined by output, and the use of electric driven machinery is the key to the maximum of production with the minimum of effort. It is the secret of successful industrial organisation.

The Shannon is being harnessed to enable the Irish industrialist and the Irish worker to use that key.

Shannon electricity will lift the heavy work of industry from human shoulders to the iron shoulders of machines.

The Great Southern Railways are issuing return tickets at single fares (available for 3 days) from all stations to Limerick. Conducted tours daily by I.O.C. buses. Permits for private parties issued on application to The Guide Bureau, Strand Barracks, Limerick.

THE ELECTRICITY SUPPLY BOARD

An advertisement published in 1928 to attract visitors to Ardnacrusha

101

horse, as was the refined thing to do in Irish duelling circles. Cosby requested that they settle their affairs on foot, however, and Burke agreed.

While removing his spurs, having dismounted, he was run through and killed by the dastardly Cosby. This led to the stories of the Castleconnell keep being haunted. As Mr Holmes wrote to the See of Armagh in 1640: 'I heard noises, sometimes of drums and trumpets sounding and other curious music with heavenly voices, then fearful screeches. . .'

Not a place to delay.

With Castleconnell behind – O'Briensbridge, Birdhill and Millbrook too – the Treaty City is approached. The hydro-electric station of Ardnacrusha, completed in 1927, is passed as the Shannon reminds us that she has more than a pretty face. Soon too she acquires something of an international status through her townlands of Annabeg, Gurrane, Drumroe and Shravokee. The collective name for these is Plassy, a name which represents to the Limerickman what the Mardyke is to the Corkonian, what the Strawberry Beds are to the Dubliner. It is a favourite beauty-spot, a tranquil place in which to sport, play or utter words of love to one of the city beauties celebrated by poet and rhymer as the fairest in the land.

Back in 1760, property was purchased there by Robert Clive who hoped this would qualify him for an Irish peerage. He had also purchased lands in Tullyglass, Rineanna, Bunratty, Drumgeely and a few houses in Limerick itself. He became known as Baron Clive of Plassy.

All this land-acquisition came about because Clive had not been awarded a title for his services to the empire. Britain and France were fighting for commercial dominance in the unstable continent of India where the Mogul empire was disintegrating. Siraj-ud-Daulah, the Nawab, had captured the British garrison in Calcutta and one of his henchmen locked 146 of them in the infamous Black Hole. Clive recaptured Calcutta and finally defeated the Nawab outside the city – at a place called Plassey. So a peaceful spot near Shannon reflects a significant event in world history.

Not for the gentle Bard of Thomond these thoughts of wars and speculations, however, Michael Hogan's muse was concerned only with 'The Beauties of Plassy':

> On the bright lawns of Plassy green April is glowing,
> By her grand woods the Shannon is gloriously flowing,
> And the young-budding leaves on the mossy boughs ring,
> With the golden-toned air-notes of sunny-eyed Spring:
> The spirit of love from the fountains of heaven,
> Light, beauty, and soul, to the landscape is given;

And the flowerets look up to the work-smiling skies,
With bright tears of sweet, silent thanks in their eyes.

...

Sweet Plassy! my fond muse were proud of her duty,
Could she weave in her wild song one beam of thy beauty!
But God did so brightly and richly array thee!
'Tis an angel alone that could praise or portray thee!
Thou seem'st as if, on deep Shannon's green border,
Nature's first glowing signet of beauty and order,
Was set upon thee, when from chaos upborne,
Earth roll'd in the beams of the first golden morn!

'Beams of the first golden morn'? So why not a dawn approach to the Treaty city which has benefited from the Shannon's wealth to an extent that **brought** about a satellite town called after the noble lady. Dawn is the time for workers to head for Shannon town's new industries. A good time too for visitors to wave to them and move on to the lady Shannon's final river crossing.

Limerick

TREATING SHANNON as an elegant lady presents the likelihood of coming across a display of fickleness and what better place to enjoy this attribute than in Limerick, originally a Danish settlement. There also stood Kincora which bred Brian Boru who finally vanquished the same Vikings from the land.

A city granted its first charter by King John of England back in 1197, Luimneach has a distinguished history; and the Shannon is about to resist the temptation to dwell at length on that history. Tossing her fickle head, she approaches the city's first bridge and relates a tale that never graced the pages of a serious history book.

Forty-nine years before the coming of Christ, Julius Caesar led his armies across the Rubicon. This event remained the most famous river-crossing of all time – until Seán a' Scuab crossed the Shannon by Limerick's Thomond Bridge many hundreds of years later, to become fabled for verbal aptitude

Treaty Stone, Thomond Bridge, King John's Castle and the River Shannon at Limerick

with a single pithy remark.

A besom or broom-maker from Cratloe, Seán acquired his nick-name from his modest profession. He marketed his products in Limerick where he repaired each Saturday with his week's output slung on his back.

It came to pass that Limerick's city fathers could not agree on a new mayor nor could an election bring about a decisive result. Perplexed, they decided on a novel form of selection to instal their first citizen. The earliest man across Thomond Bridge on a certain Saturday morning would be their mayor.

That man was Seán a' Scuab and he was duly received with great ceremony by the honorable aldermen. He was given a bit of a wash and his worn rags were replaced by robes of scarlet trimmed with ermine. The mayoral chain was hung about his neck and the city mace shoved into his trembling hand. He took his oath of office and retired for the night as Shannonside citizens decorated their beloved city for the great investiture parade next day.

Meanwhile, back in Cratloe, Seán's wife worried about his whereabouts. Thinking that he had been carousing she set out next morning to find her beloved, if bedevilled, husband. She took little notice of the gay bunting that bedecked the city's streets, but she was forced to step on to the sidewalk as the flagbearers and the prancing cavalry and the military band heralded the approach of the gilded coach pulled by six of the whitest horses she had ever seen. The crowds cheered to the new mayor who was now well pleased with himself as he waved his appreciation of their enthusiasm.

Then his wife recognised Seán. Temporarily smitten with disbelief, she recovered in time to call to her husband. He attempted to ignore her. 'Seán, a grá, it's your wife. Don't you know me at all?' Then came Sean's famous reply:

'Get away home out of that, woman. Can't you see I don't even know myself.'

The first Sunday of Lent was called Chalk Sunday in many parts of Ireland, including Limerick. On that day the backs of bachelors were marked with chalk (usually stealthily while they knelt in prayer at Mass). Like many mischievous acts, the custom sometimes got out of hand. Seldom was this more so than on Sunday 2 March 1879 at an Irishtown laneway named Clampett's Bow, where prostitutes were more plentiful than bachelors, and more violent too.

Rioting raged all day after a young man resented being 'chalked' and trounced the perpetrator of the act. Sides were taken and during the course of the fracas that followed a boy and girl were seriously injured before order was restored for a while. However, before the evening sun set on Shannon,

Clampett's Bow, John Street and surrounding areas were the scenes of pitched battles between rival factions and against the constabulary.

The *Limerick Chronicle* reported: 'In the evening word came to the police in Clare Street station that a row of a very serious nature was taking place at the head of John Street. Head Constable Phelan and all the forces available under his command immediately proceeded to the scene of the occurrence. . . but the fugitives managed to get into Moran's house. A sledge-hammer was, after some delay, procured to break in the door, but before they could even approach within a yard of it a volley of stones, bricks and bottles were thrown at them from the top garret of the building in which the besieged located themselves, and so incessant was the downpour that the police had to desist and retire under an archway. . . The police then attempted to force their way by placing tables over their heads but the protection was not sufficient and they were again forced to retreat. It was decided to surround the building and an additional force was sent for to the William Street Station.

'Up to ten o'clock. . . [the next] morning the besieged successfully defied the police to arrest them. Mr McCarthy R.M. who had been sent for at an early hour, requested the parties to surrender but they refused to do so and said that if any members of the constabulary dared to approach the house, they would stone them to death. It should be stated that the house in which the besieged were located is at the bottom of a lane so narrow that two men could hardly walk abreast when passing through it. Mr McCarthy and the Mayor held a consultation in reference to the matter, and directed the police to guard the house until ten o'clock in the morning when the house would be forcibly entered if the occupants continued to resist the law. This contingency did not arise as at ten o'clock (that evening) it was discovered that the birds had flown. They managed, it would appear, to escape through a hole in the roof. . .'

During proceedings that followed there were charges, counter-charges, lies and blasphemies. The siege may not have received the acclaim accorded to Limerick's more famous battles but at least one poet, Thomas Stanley Tracey, wrote a satirical epic.

> Oh! murder, blood and thunder
> Are the muses dead, I wonder?
> Those fine old ancient maidens
> That once lit the poet's glow.
> Are our bards all gone to blazes
> That none will sing the praises
> Of the City of the Sieges
> And the Siege of Clampett's Bow?

There's many a fight and ruction
That causes more destruction
But was ever one more striking?
The never a one I know,
Except that siege more glorious
When Limerick was victorious
And when women fought for Sarsfield
And Ireland, long ago.

...

Sure the neighbourhood of John Street,
Is immortalised by one street,
Where our heroes, on Chalk Sunday,
Did march forth to meet the foe;
When the baton-wielding police
Were routed holus-polus,
With stones and broken bottles
By the boys of Clampett's Bow.

...

Then hurrah for drink and fightin'
And the sprees we take delight in,
And the good old times when constables
Were rare as summer snow;
With John Jameson to free us
And the Clampett boys to lead us,
We'll never want such laurels
As we won at Clampett's Bow.

Leitch Ritchie prefaces a story of Mungret, close to the city, with a discourse on clergymen which is of great sociological interest. He follows it with an even more intriguing study of Limerick in the early nineteenth century.

'As a means of civilising the people, the Catholic church in Ireland has been an utter failure; its priests have contented themselves with bringing up their flocks in blind and ignorant belief, without an attempt to expand their intellect, or extend their knowledge; and at this moment, although well aware of their real wants, they use such influence as they possess in stirring up the miserable creatures to a political agitation which has no reference whatever to these wants. A political priest, of any denomination, is the most odious and mischievous of all animals — and, even if found in religious Scotland, he should be swept out of the temple he profanes, as with a besom; but what shall we say of him in Ireland, where the claims of God and nature upon his time and zeal are so numerous and so urgent? I do not venture to affirm that the diminished influence of the priesthood in Ireland is an evidence of the increased progress of education; but I do say that henceforward the one will be found to go on in an exact ratio with the other.

'As for the Protestant clergymen, on the other hand, they are in general *gentlemen*. They do not seek association with the ragged and filthy inmates of the hut. They mind their farms; exchange dinners with their respectable neighbours; lead regular lives; and die with the reputation of having performed worthily the duties of Christian priests. The presence of such men, with their families, is doubtless a great advantage to the country. They set a good moral and farming example, and spend a decent income in the district.

'The learning of the priests, I have hinted, is purely theological; and so are their manners. The habits of a secluded student engrafted on the rudeness of a clown, are not very attractive; and perhaps this is the true reason why the priests mingle but little in good society, even of their own religious persuasion. However this may be, their learning itself, independently of other proof, is pleasantly illustrated by an anecdote related of the priory of Mungret, within the liberties of Limerick.

'A deputation, it seems was sent from the College of Cashel, to try the skill of the Mungret scholars in the dead languages; and the monks were thrown into some alarm lest anything might happen to injure the reputation they had so long enjoyed. After consulting together, they dressed some of their most accomplished pupils like peasant girls, and sending them out, one by one, desired them to reply in Latin to any question that might be put to them. One of them speedily fell in with the Cashel professors, who, on asking the distance to Mungret, were startled by receiving the reply in a dead language. This happened again, and again, and again; and at length the holy fathers determined not to venture upon any examination of professors in a district where even the peasant girls spoke Latin, and turning hastily round, made their way back to Cashel.

'I have talked of the trade, the wealth, the beauty of Limerick – in fact, of the outside; and this is all which is likely to catch the eye of the cursory visitor, and all which he cares to examine. We have seen that there are numerous individuals enjoying an income of nearly a thousand pounds a year; and that there is abundance of genteel equipages, good houses and handsome women. Like the Diable Bioteux, we have unreefed the city of the busy, the gay, and the fair; and, like him, have left closely covered up the abodes of hunger and destitution. Limerick however, has not, like other great towns, merely the mixture of poverty and wealth found in all the crowded haunts of mankind.

108

Limerick, in a word, is not a town of Europe, or Asia, or Africa, or America: it is an Irish town.

'If I had contented myself with traversing Newtown, and the principal thoroughfares of Englishtown, and Irishtown, I should have pursued my journey with favourable impressions of the condition and character of the inhabitants. Then I should have seen only a fair intermixture (for an Irish town) of rags with embroidery, of hovels with houses, of concave and convex cheeks. Then I should have been as much amused as pained – may God forgive me for the hardness of heart! – by the absurd devices occasionally detected for appearing to cover the body with raiment – by the transformation of women into men, and men into women, and children into either.

'But, unhappily, I would needs calculate that the crowds I saw could be only specimens of a few thousands of the inhabitants; and I would needs diverge from the great thoroughfares of business and pleasure, to plunge into the lanes, and alleys and courts, for the purpose of looking at the remaining classes.'

If Mr Ritchie avoided the lanes and alleys, present day visitors would be well advised to explore them for therein dwell people who, although urbanised, still treasure tales of the past. They are generous in passing on their precious lore, some of which is contained in imposing volumes as well as in humble heads.

St Mary's Bells

Halls' Ireland or, to be precise, *Ireland – its Scenery, Character, &c.* by Mr & Mrs S. C. Hall is one of those beautifully bound, gold-edged books laden with tissued illustrations that bibliolaters love to caress. It contains a delightful footnote elaborating on its reference to St Mary's Cathedral, built on the site of the palace of O'Brien, King of Thomond, and founded by Donal Mór O'Brien after the 1176 fire of Limerick. The Halls said the edifice was the only place from which a good view of the city could be seen and their story ends with a picture of that very panorama:

'There is a curious and interesting tradition connected with the bells of Limerick cathedral. The story is prettily told, and will bear repetition. They were, it is said, brought originally from Italy, where they were manufactured by a young native, who grew justly proud of the successful results of years of anxious toil expanded in their production. They were subsequently purchased by the prior of a neighbouring convent; and with the profits of this sale the young Italian procured a little villa, where he had the pleasure of hearing the tolling of his bells from the convent cliff, and of growing old in the bosom of domestic happiness. This, however, was not to continue. In some of those

109

St Mary's Cathedral

broils, whether civil or foreign, which are the undying worm in the peace of a fallen land, the good Italian was a sufferer amongst many. He lost his all; and, after the passing of the storm, found himself preserved alone amid the wreck of fortune, friends, family and home. The convent in which the bells, the *chiefs-d'oeuvre* of his skill, were hung, was razed to the earth, and the bells were carried away to another land. The unfortunate owner, haunted by his memories, and deserted by his hopes, became a wanderer over Europe. His hair grew grey, and his heart withered, before he again found a home and a friend. In this desolation of spirit, he formed the resolution of seeking the place to which the treasures of his memory had been finally borne. He sailed for Ireland, proceeded up the Shannon; the vessel anchored in the pool near Limerick, and he hired a small boat for the purpose of landing. The city was now before him; and he beheld St Mary's steeple, lifting its turreted head above the smoke and mist of the old town. He sat in the stern, and looked fondly towards it. It was an evening so calm and beautiful as to remind him of his own native haven in the sweetest time of the year – the death of the spring.

'The broad stream appeared like one smooth mirror, and the little vessel glided through it. On a sudden, amid the general stillness, the bells tolled from the cathedral; the rowers rested on their oars, and the vessel went forward with the impulse it had received. The aged Italian looked towards the city, crossed arms on his breast, and lay back in his seat; home, happiness, early recollections, friends, family – all were in the sound, and went with it to his heart. When the rowers looked round, they beheld him with his face still turned towards the cathedral; but his eyes were closed, and when they landed they found him dead!'

A little of the Bard of Thomond's poem, *The Silver Bells* must be quoted here. It concerns another legend of St Mary's Bells, when friars hid them from marauding 'reformers', but its introductory lines serve for either story:

> The bright-red even' is purpling o'er
> The golden summits of Cappantimore,
> And the dark-blue Shannon is rolling down
> By the war-cleft ramparts of Limerick town.
> There roams no zephyr on bank or shore –
> The hills are hazed and the plains are hoar;
> And the moss-clad bridge with its rocky chain
>   Of hurl-built arches, lay o'er the tide,
> And its brown shadow rusted the silver plain
>   Of the sweeping current from side to side;
> While the sunset cloudlets seem'd to diffuse,

In the river's crystal, their diamond hues,
    As if spirits were lining its bed below,
With the glistening dyes of the showery bow.
On bank and mead, town, turret and wood,
A calm, like the charm of dreamland, dwells,
And nothing is heard but the hoarse-toned flood,
    And the golden chime of St Mary's bells.

Sarsfield

Sarsfield went out, the Dutch to rout,
And to take and break their cannon;
To Mass went he at half-past-three
And at four he crossed the Shannon.

Aubrey de Vere was not the only poet who made Patrick Sarsfield his subject. The warrior immortalised for his action against King William's siege train at Ballyneety has been a recurring source of pride for generations of authors and historians.

Fine English was once a status-symbol in rural Ireland. That was when Gaelic lived on as the language of the common folk even as it was considered a sign of having received an education if a word or two of the King's English dropped from tea-stained lips. Foolish young men learned phrases at the behest of sorely pressed matchmakers and there was little to beat a good prognostication of proving pluvial or the like in bidding for a fair fortune if

Patrick Sarsfield

112

not a fair figure. This trait lingered in men of the soil long after English — through great misfortune and greater carelessness — became the spoken language. Sons of gombeen men still used fine words to impress and so it came to pass that a young student of the forties entered a diocesan seminary and was asked to write an essay or 'composition'. The subject was Patrick Sarsfield.

Now this boy had broken everything on his father's farm except the crowbar and he bent that. Realising he was fit only for the priesthood, therefore, the father had instilled in the lad the importance of the 'turn of phrase'. A great *glaum* reached for an N-pen. He would show some of these smart townie class-mates with scholarships and red boots a thing or two! He would impress the professor of English. Right! Patrick Sarsfield, paragraph one: 'The sun was slowly sinking in a crimson fresnel as the siege train shunted into Ballyneety. . .'

Commentators on the Shannon's lore and loveliness often finish their discourse at Limerick, forgetting that the river's fine estuary extends, arguably, to a line between Loop Head and Kerry Head. Goodly folk there are in Kerry and south Clare who rightly consider themselves claimants to some of Shannon's fame. Heading hence, the Bard of Thomond again provides fitting verse:

> . . . Farewell! to thy old hospitable halls,
>   And veteran ramparts now no longer ours!
> Farewell to thy invulnerable walls —
>   Thy festive palaces and lordly towers!
> Farewell! to thy all-beauteous, bright-eyed maids,
>   Whose deeds shall long be honour'd and admired —
> The stranger now may revel in thy shades,
>   Where Freedom, in her last retreat, expired!
>
> Far o'er the heavings of the angry deep,
>   I'll meet thy foes upon another shore!
> My sword shall yet a vengeful harvest reap,
>   For Sarsfield's last brave battle is not o'er!
> Limerick! one grateful boon from thee I claim —
>   Whatever fate holds bright or dark for me —
> That thou wilt cherish faithful Sarsfield's name,
>   And love his memory as he loved thee!

The only angry deep the traveller crosses is the Feale, the only foe is time, which denies a longer visit.

Lower Shannon

'THIS DIVISION comprehends what may be termed the marine portion of the Shannon, which extends from the mouth of the river up to Limerick, and from the confluence of the Fergus with the Shannon, to the village of Clare, two miles below the town of Ennis. . .'

So says the *Second Report of the Commissioners for the Improvement of the Navigation of the River Shannon* dated 9 December 1837. This would bring the western end just about to where Shannon airport is now. The report continues: 'First, the great sea estuary extending from Kilkadrane and Bale Points (assumed, for all practical purposes, to be the western limits of the river), to Grass Island, 15 miles below Limerick; comprising a distance of 60 miles. . .'

Disappointment looms for some Kerrymen below Kilconly Point near Ballybunion and the Claremen south of Carrigaholt. But wait!: 'In fixing upon Kilkadrane and Bale Points as the virtual entrance of the Shannon, we have adopted these points arbitrarily.'

> 'My son,' he said, 'be not afraid,
>   I am the Genius of this tide!
> And often, on my summer banks,
>   I heard thy swelling strains, with pride!
> Now from my weedy palace-caves
>   I came to tell a tale of wrong. . .'

The Bard of Thomond's tale is not the only tale of wrong associated with this part of the Shannon. Here is also the location for Gerald Griffin's fine novel *The Collegians*. This classic novel, based on the facts of the Scanlan murder case of 1819, was the inspiration for Dion Boucicault's play *The Colleen Bawn* in 1860. The novel tells the sad story of the murder of the beautiful Eily O'Connor of Garryowen, a rope-maker's daughter.

She leaves her home because of her father's insistance on her marriage with Myles Murphy — Myles na Coppaleen. But the lovely Eily is already secretly married. The involved plot leads to Eily's sad departure from where she spent her wedding-night shortly before she is drowned in the Shannon.

The author paints a gentle picture: 'Eily, as if yielding to a mechanical

Gerald Griffin from a portrait by Richard Rothwell

impulse, glided into the little room, which, during the honeymoon, had been furnished up and decorated for her own use. She restrained her eyes from wandering as much as possible, and commenced with hurried and trembling hands her arrangements for departure. They were few and speedily effected. Her apparel was folded into her trunk, and for once she tied on her bonnet and cloak without referring to the glass. It was all over now! It was a happy dream, but it was ended. . .'

Not yet ended, thankfully, is the Shannon's happy dream, even if signs of departure are evident. The estuary narrows somewhat. Labasheeda beckons from a curvature of south Clare and across the water stands Foynes.

The Commissioners for the Improvement of the River Shannon had much to say of Foynes in their Second Report presented to both Houses of Parliament by Command of Her Majesty in 1837. These 'humble servants', J. F. Burgoyne, Harry D. Jones and Richard Griffith, had just recommended that all timber used in their proposed piers should be Kyanised despite the fact that timber covered by Shannon's waters was never attacked by *Teredo Navalis* or other destructive marine insects. They added: 'The harbour of Foynes, on the south side of the river, is situated ten miles to the eastward of Tarbert. This place affords excellent shelter from all winds, being protected from the south and west by high lands adjoining the river bank, and from the north and north-east by Foynes Island. The harbour, in fact, consists of the

The Courthouse in which the Scanlan murder trial took place

116

Foynes

channel that separates Foynes Island and the mainland, in which there is an ample depth of water at all times of tide.

'Foynes is well situated as a converging point for the traffic of the north-western portion of the county of Limerick; an extensive district, not many years since the scene of lawless disturbance and agricultural inactivity, but now happily under rapid transition into one of peace, industry and prosperity. The new roads, made principally at the public expense, have tended in a great measure to this striking improvement, and a facility of export for the constantly increasing agricultural products of the country is much required; this can be effected most advantageously by the erection of a shipping wharf at Foynes, in a situation affording peculiar facilities for the purpose, where there is ample depth of water, a sheltered anchorage, an extensive platform in the rear of it, close to the high road between Limerick and Tarbert, and within 1,100 yards of one of the finest limestone quarries in the south of Ireland.'

The gentlemen then submitted plans and an estimate amounting to £8,500. The plans, 'shewing the Course of the Tide' and giving detailed soundings, cross sections of jetties and the like are works of art in themselves.

117

'The Clare' landing at Foynes

'Piggy-back' aircraft at Foynes

118

Aubrey de Vere's brother Stephen is buried in Foynes. With William Smith O'Brien's daughter Charlotte, he was prominent in denouncing the infamous coffin-ships that transported starving emigrants to America in the time of the famine. Foynes and nearby Glin were featured in the ferrying of IRA Volunteers across the Shannon when they were forced to go on the run during the War of Independence. And then, there came more plans and more reports as a native government kept pace with the times and established the nation's first commercial Trans-Atlantic air route from its seaplane base at Foynes. That was in 1939. These particular waters of Shannon have served the nation well.

Sacred Scattery

During the sixth century, the misogynist St Senanus founded a monastery on Scattery Island where he is said to have built eleven churches. The place was always regarded with some respect and a little awe. Estuary fishermen were reluctant to sail a craft that had not completed a round of Scattery into a setting sun or put to sea without some pebbles from the island aboard. Its holy well was highly regarded by the faithful. People afraid to cross the water to make a pilgrimage there 'paid a Scattery prayer'; that is, they paid another pilgrim to make their spiritual Odyssey for them. There was said to have been at least one professional pilgrim who worked full time at this proxy petitioning.

Scattery Island

119

After his death about 560, St Senanus is said to have stood in his coffin to exhort his monks to pray and be hospitable. Before resuming his recumbent posture he named his successor.

In *The Shannon and its Lakes,* Richard Harvey wrote: 'It is an island in the barony of Moyarta, County Clare, Munster. It lies in the Shannon, one mile and three-quarters south-south-west of Kilrush, and three-quarters of a mile south of the nearest part of the mainland. It contains about 100 acres: the soil good, well stocked with cattle, and abounding with rabbits and wild fowl; but though inhabited, its population is not specially returned. It is a low-browed island, remarkable for hardly anything in its configuration or natural structure and produce; yet when its size and physical insignificance are considered, it figures so prominently in history and archaeology as to be one of the wonders of Ireland. Its sound or roadstead was early ascertained by the Vikings to be one of their most convenient harbours for making descents upon Ireland; and the island, in consequence, was for a long period a bone of contention and a scene of strife between them and the Irish. In 975, Brian Boromh, at the head of 1,200 Dalgais troops, and assisted by Domnhall, King of Toamhuein, recovered the island from the Danes, by defeating their leader Tomhar and his two sons in a pitched battle, and slaying in the strife 800 of the Danes who had fled to the place for protection.

'Owing to this and other battles, and still more perhaps to its having been for many ages a favourite burying-place, the whole island is strewed some feet deep with human bones; and in some places where the sea has worn down the shore to a mural face or mimic perpendicular cliff, a stratum of human bones is visible six or seven feet from the surface. At a later and more peaceable period, the merchants of Limerick had castles and stone dwelling-houses on the island, "with a provost or warden, who might dispend 100 marks yearly". In the reign of Henry VIII, Edmund Sexton recommended it as a proper site for a fortress, which, with one ship of sixty guns, and two or three galleys, would overawe all the territory which now forms the counties of Clare, Limerick, Kerry, and Cork; and, even in our day, it figures as a strong military ground, or at least as the site of a small fort.

'But Inniscattery, after all, owes its main importance to its ecclesiastical antiquities and associations. An alleged bishopric is said to have been established on it by St Patrick, and to have been governed for a time by himself, and then transferred to St Senanus; and this supposed bishopric is asserted to have been united in the twelfth century to the See of Limerick. St Senanus, who makes the principal figure in whatever relates to the ecclesiastical associations of the island, is nearly as phantasmagorial a personage as St Kevin of Glendalough, and forms the subject of probably as many and as wild legendary tales; but, on the whole, he may be described, according to the picture of him by credulous admirers, as having been so chaste a monk as never to look at a woman, or suffer one to be on the island, and so zealous a propagator of monasticism as to found many monasteries in Munster.

Ballybunion

Mr and Mrs Hall wrote of this area: 'The Main-coach road from Tralee to Limerick passes through the town of Listowel, and that of Tarbert; the former being inland, the latter on the South bank of the Shannon. The far-famed caves of Ballybunian are about an equal distance from both, but on the coast. Listowel is a poor town, with, of course, the ruins of a castle. In the year 1600 this castle, which held out for Lord Kerry against the Lord President, was besieged by Sir Charles Wilmot. Listowel is watered by the Feal, a river which the Irish poet has immortalised in one of the sweetest of his songs; founded on a tradition, that the young heir of the princely Desmonds, having been benighted while hunting, took shelter in the house of one of his dependants, named MacCormac; with whose fair daughter he became suddenly enamoured. "He married her; and by this inferior alliance alienated his followers, whose brutal pride regarded this indulgence of his love as an unpardonable degradation of his family." The story rests on the authority of Leland; the poet makes the lord thus address his rebellious clan:

> You who call it dishonour
> To bow to this flame,
> If you've eyes, look but on her,
> And blush while you blame.
> Hath the pearl less witness
> Because of its birth?
> Hath the violet less brightness
> For growing near earth?

'The caves of Ballybunian are not often visited; yet they may be classed among the most remarkable of the natural wonders of Ireland. The old historian alludes to them very briefly: "The whole shore here hath a variety of romantic caves and caverns, formed by the dashing of the waves; in some places are high open arches, and in others impending rocks, ready to tumble down upon the first storm"; a small volume descriptive of them was, however, published in 1834, by William Ainsworth, Esq.; to which we must refer the reader. They are distinguished by names, each name bearing reference to some particular circumstance, as "The Hunter's Path", from a

Cliff scenery, Ballybunion

tradition that a rider once rode his horse over it; "Smugglers' Bay", for centuries famous as a safe shelter for "free traders"; the "Seal Cave", &c. &c.'

A footnote attributed to the aforementioned William Ainsworth says: 'The cliffs of Ballybunian are even less remarkable for their dimensions than they are for the singular form of rocks, which seem as if carved by the hand of man; and, independently of the lofty mural precipices, whose angular proportions present every variety of arrangement, as in Smugglers' Bay, where they often-times are semi-circularly arranged, like the grain-work of an arch, or the tablets or small strings running round a window, or are piled above one another in regular succession, presenting a geological phenomenon of great grandeur and magnificence; they have also other distinct beauties, which originate frequently in similar causes.'

In more recent times, Ballybunion has been better known as a place for country people to go for holiday and sport. Listowel's renowned writer John B. Keane wrote an interesting play about them called *The Buds of Ballybunion*. The final lines from that work provide a nostalgic farewell:

Goodbye to Ballybunion where the green seas ebb and flow,
Goodbye to every lofty cliff and golden sands below.
Farewell, farewell my only love, the time has come to go,
Goodbye to Ballybunion and the Buds of long ago.

Headlands

The perpetrators of the Kerryman joke might be surprised at Leitch Ritchie's observations on the inhabitants of the land around what the ordnance survey map called *The Mouth of Shannon*: 'From Tarbert to Tralee the journey is not interesting in its physical features; although the curious traveller will be struck by the difference observable in the air and physiognomy of the people. The tradition which bears that the sea-coast of Kerry was peopled from Spain can hardly be erroneous, since a confirmatory proof appears in almost every face you see... The Kerry peasant has a dignity of his own, far better than that of all the nobility in the world – a dignity arising from the sense of independence. There is no Spanish laziness about him; and, what is still better, no Spanish flightiness. He works hard and lives sparingly; and he goes forward to his task with an energy of purpose altogether unknown to his continental cousins...'

We have now come to the end of our journey. Shannon's mouth forms into a smile as her lips at Loop Head and Kerry Head part for a last farewell kiss. The parting is like the leaving of any good woman. Her breath invites a longer

Loop Head

stay, her beauty more exploration. Relaxed and stretched, her great estuary unobstrusively has become sea.

There is no distinct point at which river changes to ocean – just as there is no precise moment when feminine serenity becomes abandoned passion. It is a slow and subtle modulation, never without appeal, ever ecstatic.

And just as the departing lover promises to return to his mistress, so too the Shannon's seduction brings the vow of a further visit.

> 'Tis, it is the Shannon's stream
> Brightly glancing, brightly glancing,
> See, oh, see the ruddy beam
> Upon its waters dancing!
> Thus returned from travel vain,
> Years of exile, years of pain,
> To see old Shannon's face again,
> Oh, the bliss entrancing!

124

Bibliography

Unpublished Sources, Reports, Journals, Magazines etc.

Manuscripts of the Department of Irish Folklore, University College, Dublin.
Stories collected from rivermen etc.
Private documents of James Fanning, *Midland Tribune*, Birr.
Private documents of Kathleen Mullally, Mullingar.
An Cosantoir, Defence Forces Journal.
The Irish Sword, Military History Society of Ireland Journal, Vol. VIII, Vol. XI.
Ireland, Fogra Fáilte publication.
Teathbha, Journal of Longford Historical Society, Vol. I.
Breifne, Vol. III, No. 9.
Leitrim Guardian Yearbook 1979
Old Limerick Journal, Old Limerick Society publication, 1978, 1980.
Parliamentary Gazetteer of Ireland 1844-45.
Geographical Distribution of Ireland Ability (1812 Report).
The Irish Statesman, March 1926.
Report on Concord Lodge 834, Carrick-on-Shannon 1797-1897 by Abraham O'Connor, Past Provincial and Senior Grand Warden, North Connaught.
Banagher– a brief history published by Banagher Parish Council 1951.
Report on an *Inquiry into the Extent and Cause of Shannon Floods* ordered by Treasury minute dated 30 May 1862. Letter of instruction concerning same.
The Other Clare, Shannon Archaelogical and Historical Journal Vol. 4.
Register of Baptisms, Marriages and Burials for Killaloe Parish 1698.
Manuscript Documents of Longford Historical Society Archives.
Report of the Commissioners for the Improvement of the Shannon Navigation 1837.
Document entitled 'A True and Impartial History of the Most Material Occurrences in the Kingdom of Ireland 1693'.
The Journal of the Ardagh and Clonmacnois Antiquarian Society 1951.
Extracts from the journal of Thomas Dineley Esquire giving an account of his visit to Ireland in the reign of Charles II.
Shannon Navigation Bill 1874.
Letter to *Daily News* 1874 (21 October).
News reports from *Leitrim Observer, Longford Leader, Roscommon Herald, Westmeath-Offaly Independent, Midland Tribune, Clare Champion, Limerick Chronicle.*
References from *Book of Leinster, Book of Armagh, Book of Ballymote, Annals of the Four Masters.*

Extracts from poems by:

John Keegan Casey, Richard Dalton Williams, Aubrey de Vere, Percy French, John Keaveney, Thomas d'Arcy McGee, Myles McTigue, James Clarence Mangan, Susan Langstaff Mitchell, Padraic O'Farrell, Theophilus O'Flynn, Michael Hogan, Gerald Griffin, M. J. McCann.

Works consulted

Burleth, Richard. *The Twilight Lords*. Allen Lane, London 1978.
Boylan, Henry. *A Dictionary of Irish Biography*. Gill & Macmillan, Dublin 1978.
Brown, S.J. *Ireland in Fiction*. Irish University Press, Shannon 1969.
Bulfin, William. *Rambles in Erin*, M. H. Gill, Dublin 1907.
Butler, Anthony. *The Book of Bull*. Malton Press, Dublin 1974.
Butler, Harriet J. and Butler, H. Edgeworth. eds. *The Black Book of Edgeworthstown and other Edgeworth Memories*. Faber & Gwyer, London 1925.
Cahill, Susan and Thomas. *A Literary Guide to Ireland*. Wolfhound Press, Dublin 1979.
Carleton, William. *Tales and Sketches... of the Irish Peasantry*. Duffy, Dublin 1845.
Chambers, Anne, *Granuaile. The Life and Times of Grace O'Malley*. Wolfhound Press, Dublin 1979.
Clancy, Eileen and Forde, Patrick. *Ballinaglera Parish*. Private (Printed Argus Press, Dublin), 1980.
Clancy, Peter. *Historical Notices of the Parish of Inishmagrath*. Private, 1958.
Colum, Padraic. *A Treasury of Irish Folklore*. Crown, New York 1967.
Cowan, John. *Description of the Upper Part of the River Shannon*. J. and J. Carrick (Printers), Dublin 1795.
Cowan, John. *Survey of the Entire Course of the River Shannon* Private, 1773.
Craig, Maurice and the Knight of Glin. *Ireland Observed*. The Mercier Press, Dublin and Cork 1980.
Delany, D. R. *The Canals of the South of Ireland,* David & Charles, London 1966.
Edgeworth, Maria and Richard. *Essays of Irish Bulls,* J. Johnson, London 1803.
Edgeworth, Maria and Richard. *Practical Education*. J. Johnson, London 1798.
Edgeworth, Maria. *Castle Rackrent*. J. Johnson, London , 1814.
Edgeworth, Maria. *The Absentee*. Macmillan, London 1809.
Edgeworth, Maria, *Belinda*. Baldwin and Craddock, London 1833.
Fallis, Richard. *The Irish Renaissance*. Gill & Macmillan, Dublin 1978.
Farrell, J. P. *Historical Notes of County Longford*. Dollard, Dublin 1886.
Farrell, J. P. *History of County Longford*. Dollard, Dublin 1891. (Reprinted, *Longford Leader,* Longford 1980).
Feehan, John M. *The Magic of the Shannon*. The Mercier Press, Dublin and Cork 1980.
French, Percy. *Poems, Prose and Parodies*. Talbot Press, Dublin 1925.
Gardener, Raymond. *Land of Time Enough,* Hodder & Stoughton, London 1977.
Girouard, Mark. *Life in the English Country House*. Yale, London 1978.
Gmelch, Sharon, ed. *Irish Life*. O'Brien Press, Dublin 1979.
Goldsmith, Oliver. *She Stoops to Conquer. The Deserted Village: Goldsmith's Choice Works,* W. P. Nimmo, Hay & Mitchell, Edinburgh (n.d.).

Griffin, Gerald. *The Collegians*. Talbot Press, Dublin 1953. *Select Poems of Gerald Griffin*. M. H. Gill & Son, Dublin 1903.

Hall, Rev. James. *Tour Through Ireland*, London 1913.

Hall, Mr & Mrs S. C. *Ireland, its scenery, characters &c. (Hall's Ireland)*. How & Parsons, London, Vol.I.

Hardiman, Thomas. *Hardiman's History of Galway*. Dublin 1820. (Reprinted by *Connaught Tribune*, Galway 1958).

Harvey, R. *The Shannon and its Lakes*. Hodges Figgis, 1896.

Hayward, Richard. *Where the River Shannon Flows*. Dundalgan Press, Dundalk (n.d.). First published George G. Harrap 1940.

Hogan, Michael. *Lays and Lagends of Thomond*. M. H. Gill & Son, Dublin 1880.

Hogan, Robert, ed. *The Macmillan Dictionary of Irish Literature*. Gill & Macmillan, Dublin 1980.

Hole, S. Reynolds. *A Little Tour of Ireland*. Edward Arnold, London 1892.

Hunt, B. *Folk Tales of Breffny*, Macmillan & Co., London 1912.

Hyde, Douglas. *A Literary History of Ireland*. F. Unwin, London 1899.

Inglis, H. D. *Ireland*. Whittaker & Co., London 1835.

Joyce, P. W. *Old Celtic Romances*. David Nutt, London 1894.

Kennedy, Patrick. *Legendary Fictions of the Irish Celts,* Macmillan, London & New York 1891.

Killanin & Duignan. *The Shell Guide to Ireland,* Ebury, London 1962.

Kinsella, Thomas. *The Tain* (Translation). Dolmen, Dublin 1969.

Larminie, William. *West Irish Folk Tales and Romances*. Irish University Press, Shannon 1972.

Lewis. *Topographical Dictionary of Ireland*. Printed by Gilbert and Rivington, London 1837.

Logan, Patrick. *The Holy Wells of Ireland*. Colin Smythe, Gerrards Cross, Bucks. 1980.

Lyons, F. S. C. *Ireland Since the Famine*. Weidenfeld & Nicolson, London 1971.

McCartney, Donal. ed.*The World of Daniel O'Connell*. The Mercier Press, Dublin & Cork 1980.

McCoy, G. A. Hayes. *Irish Battles*. Longmans, London 1969.

McCraith, L. M. *The Romance of Irish Heroines*. Longmans, London 1913.

McDonagh, Bernard, *Lough Gill*. Sligo School of Landscape Painting, Sligo (undated).

MacLysagt, Edward. *The Surnames of Ireland*. Irish Academic Press, Dublin 1978.

Mageoghan (ed. Murphy). *Annals of Clonmacnoise*. University Press, Dublin 1896.

Maxwell, Constantia, *The Stranger in Ireland*. Gill & Macmillan, Dublin 1979.

Moody & Martin. *The Course of Irish History*. The Mercier Press, Dublin & Cork 1966.

Moore, Thomas. *Prose and Verse*. Chatto & Windus, London 1878.

Neill, Kenneth. *An Illustrated History of the Irish People*. Gill & Macmillan, Dublin 1979.

O'Brien, William. *A Queen of Men*. T. Unwin Fisher, London 1898.

O'Callaghan, Michael. *To Ireland and Freedom*. Roscommon Herald, Boyle 1964.

Ó Dalaigh, Padraig, ed. *Ballad History of Ireland*. Educational Co. of Ireland, Dublin (n.d.)

O'Donovan, John. *The Tribes and Customs of Hy-Many*. Tower, Cork 1976.

Ó Dubhagain, Seán. (Hereditary bard to Eoghan O'Madden). His *Topographical Poems*. publ. Irish Archaeological and Celtic Society, Dublin 1862.

Ó Faolain, Seán. *King of the Beggars*. Poolbeg Co., Dublin 1980.

——. *The Irish*, Pelican, London 1947.

O'Farrell, Padraic. *The Mercier Book of Irish Records*. The Mercier Press, Dublin & Cork 1978.

——. *Who's Who in the Irish War of Independence 1916-1921*, The Mercier Press, 1980.

——. *How the Irish Speak English*, The Mercier Press, 1980.

——. *Bedside Book of the West of Ireland*. The Mercier Press, 1981.

——. *Life Train*. Cillenna, Dublin 1983.

O'Flaherty, Roderick. *West or H-Iar Connaught*. 1684. Notes and Illustrations by Jas. Hardiman for Irish Archaelogical Society 1846.

O'Sullivan, Seán. *The Folklore of Ireland*. Batsford, London 1974.

Rhodes, Thomas. *River Shannon Navigation. . .* Ordered by House of Commons. Dublin 1833.

Rice, H. T. *Thanks for the Memory*. Athlone Printing Works, Athlone 1952.

Ritchie, Leitch. *Ireland, Picturesque and Romantic*. Vol 2. Longman, Orme Brown, Green & Longmans, London 1838.

Rolleston, T. W. *Myths and Legends of the Celtic Race*. George Harrap, London 1916.

Rolt, L. T. C. *Green and Silver.*George Allen & Unwin, London 1949.

Sharkey, P. A. *The Heart of Ireland*. Ward, Boyle 1927,

Stephens, James. *Irish Fairy Tales*. Macmillan & Co., London 1924. (Gill & Macmillan, Dublin 1979).

Stevenson, Burton E. *The Charm of Ireland*. Dodd, Mead & Co, New York 1915.

Swan, Harry Percival. *Highlights of Ireland's Story*. Dundalgan, Dundalk 1969.

Synge, John M. *Plays, Poems and Prose*. J. M. Dent & Sons, London 1941.

Thompson, David. *Woodbrook*. Barrie & Jenkins, London 1974.

Wakefield, Edward. *An Account of Ireland, Statistical and Political*. Longman & Co., London 1812.

Wakeman, W. F. *A Week in the West of Ireland*. Hodges and Smith, Dublin 1852; *Three Days on the Shannon*. Hodges and Smith, Dublin 1852.

Walker, J. *Historical Memoirs of the Irish Bards. . .* Christie, Dublin 1818.

Weir, Anthony. *Early Ireland*. Blackstaff Press, Belfast 1980.

Weld, Isaac. *The Statistical Survey of the County Roscommon*. Royal Dublin Society, Dublin 1832.

Wilde, Lady. *Ancient Legends, Mystic Charms and Superstitions of Ireland*. Chatto & Windus, London 1919.

Wilde, William. *Irish Popular Superstitions*. Irish Academic Press, Dublin 1979.

Woods, James. *Annals of Westmeath*. Sealy, Brayers & Walker, Dublin 1907.